1 René Crevel
2 Philippe Soupault
3 Arp
4 Max Ernst
5 Max Morise
6 Fédor Dostoïevski
7 Rafaele Sanzio
8 Théodore Fraenkel
9 Paul Eluard
10 Jean Paulhan
11 Benjamin Péret
12 Louis Aragon
13 André Breton
14 Baargeld
15 Giorgio di Chirico
16 Gala Eluard
17 Robert Desnos
Décembre
1922

Uwe M. Schneede

SURREALISM

Translated by Maria Pelikan

HARRY N. ABRAMS, INC., PUBLISHERS, NEW YORK

Frontispiece: Max Ernst. *The Rendezvous of Friends.* Painted in 1922.
Oil on canvas, 3' 6 1/4" × 6' 4 3/4". Wallraf-Richartz Museum, Cologne

Library of Congress Cataloging in Publication Data

Schneede, Uwe M.
Surrealism.

(The Library of great art movements)
Translation of Malerei des Surrealismus.
Bibliography: p.
1. Surrealism. I. Title.
NX600.S9S2813 759.06 74–2302
ISBN 0-8109-1627-4 (HC)
ISBN 0-8109-2066-2 (PB)

Library of Congress Catalogue Card Number: 74–2302

Harry N. Abrams, Incorporated, New York
Printed and bound in Japan

CONTENTS

SURREALISM

COLORPLATES

THE AUTHOR REGARDS SURREALISM as a historic movement that took place between 1924 and 1939 which brought forth socio-political ideas as well as a wealth of artistic products. At times the theory and the practice of Surrealism contradicted each other. This very contradictoriness can be considered one of the characteristics of Surrealism.

Surrealist art has no common style in the traditional sense. The unifying factor in the works shown here is the use of certain methods of approach: automatic notation, the combination of incongruous elements, metamorphosis, and enigma.

The first part of this book discusses the basic criteria of Surrealist art and also the various theories and political factions within the movement. In the second part an attempt has been made to explain the way in which Surrealist principles manifest themselves in the pictures reproduced here, to show how Surrealist working methods have replaced traditional aesthetics with a wealth of contradictory variants of the basic Surrealist principles, and also to show that these principles, in various forms, have survived in today's art.

I am greatly indebted to Hans Holländer, whose essay (bibl. 46), in which he introduces the idea of incongruous combination into the analysis of Surrealism, has greatly inspired and helped my own researches. Holländer has the distinction of having applied an analytical approach to a subject which heretofore had been mainly discussed by members of the movement itself, whose critical impartiality may have been somewhat less than total.

UWE M. SCHNEEDE

SURREALISM

SURREALISM

Dada—"A Mental Attitude"

"For us, in Cologne in 1919, Dada was first of all a mental attitude . . . our aim was total subversion. A ghastly and senseless war had cheated us out of five years of our lives. We had seen all that had been held up to us as good, beautiful and true topple into an abyss of ridicule and shame. The work I produced in those days was not meant to please but to make people scream" (Max Ernst, bibl. 8).

ZURICH

Dada began in Zurich in 1916. World War I had destroyed many artists' and intellectuals' belief in the light of reason. Middle-class ideals and middle-class culture had been unmasked. Zurich, in neutral Switzerland, became a meeting place for expatriates who were no longer safe in their own countries: because they were pacifists or because they belonged to the radical left and to anarchist groups, or because their bohemian life-style made them undesirables. In 1916 a group of such cultural refugees founded the Cabaret Voltaire in Zurich. They were Jean (Hans) Arp from Alsace, Hugo Ball from Germany, and Marcel Janco and Tristan Tzara from Rumania. The Cabaret Voltaire was to be a kind of artists' meeting place with entertainment of high literary quality. As yet, the group had no clearly defined program: "Cabaret Voltaire is the name by which a group of young artists and writers have established themselves in order to create a center for artistic entertainment. Its purpose will be to have the artists who patronize the cabaret sing, dance, recite or perform their own works" (Hugo Ball, bibl. 4).

Three weeks after the Cabaret Voltaire was founded, Richard Huelsenbeck joined the circle around Hugo Ball and brought the idyllic phase of the movement to an end. Huelsenbeck, an antiwar activist and foe of middle-class culture, objected to all conformist kinds of entertainment. The cabaret's program thus began to take on a more distinctive profile. "Dada makes anticultural propaganda out of honesty, out of disgust, out of a profound distaste for the high-flown pretensions of the certified intellectuals of the bourgeoisie" (Huelsenbeck, bibl. 1). Despite their individual differences, the Dadaists had become a group.

In July 1916, the First Dada Soiree took place in the Zunfthaus zur Waag. Instead of dinner music, there were pieces by Erik Satie and Arnold Schönberg and, following the lead of Luigi Russolo, the Futurist, bruitist compositions and concerted noise. Instead of chansons, there were simultaneous poems, asyntactic noise compositions which —like the *Parole in Libertà* of 1912 by Filippo Tommaso Marinetti—anticipated Concrete Poetry. Manifestos were read in which polemic alternated with nonsense.

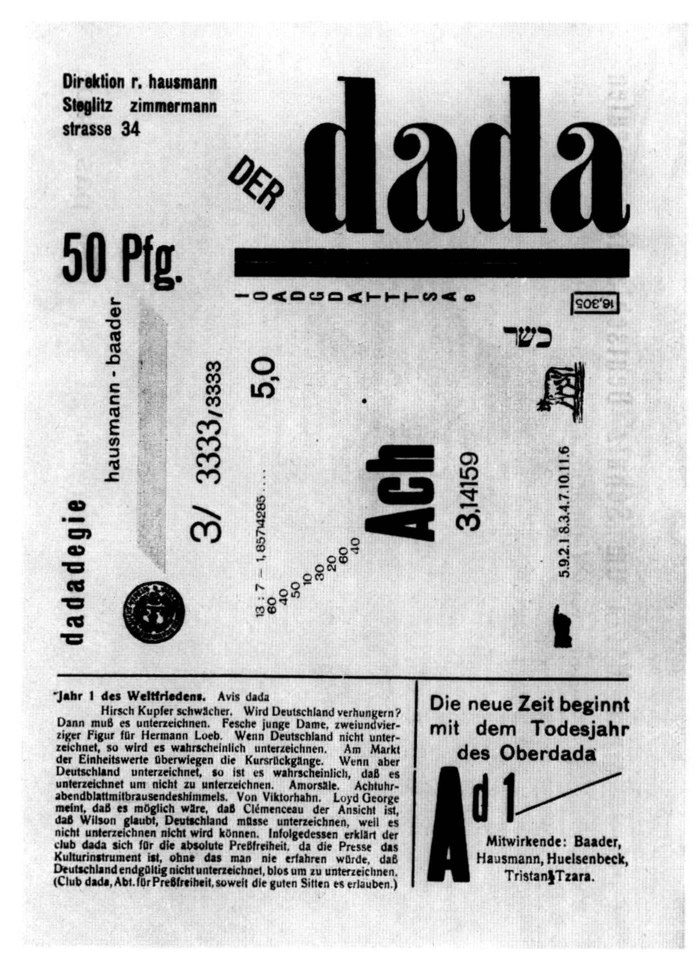

1. Cover for *Der Dada,* No. 1, Berlin, 1919

The polemical attacks were directed at everything and everybody, including the Expressionists: "Under pretense of inwardness, the Expressionists of literature and painting have merged into a generation which has begun to yearn for its own enshrinement in the history of literature and art. It has become a candidate for bourgeois honors. Under pretense of propagating the soul, they have—in their struggle against Naturalism—found their way back to those hollow abstract gestures that presume an empty, comfortable, and uneventful life" (Huelsenbeck, "Dadaist Manifesto," Berlin, 1918). Huelsenbeck advanced the opinion that Expressionism had been mentally and artistically synonymous with the "war machinery" of 1914. Arp called the Expressionists "painting-deities."

The Dada movement quickly attracted new members—some for a short period only. Among them were Viking Eggeling, Francis Picabia, Hans Richter, Christian Schad, and Walter Serner. Everything they produced, their magazines, books, exhibitions, and soirees, served the purpose of presenting "the ideals of culture and art as part of a variety show. . . . This is our kind of *Candide* against the times" (Ball, bibl. 4). The absurd, polemical, irrational performances, lectures, and dance recitals were meant to provoke the middle classes. Dadaists liked to inform and, at the same time, stir up their audiences by means of manifestos. "The manifesto as literary expression had the directness we desired. We wanted to lose no time, we wanted to provoke our enemies into action and, if necessary, make new enemies. What we hated most was romantic peace and quiet, and the search for one's soul" (Huelsenbeck, bibl. 10).

The basic political approach was Anarchism as preached by Bakunin and Kropotkin. Ball, Huelsenbeck, and Serner especially considered themselves near-anarchists, but without any precise political idea. The Dadaists subscribed to Bakunin's theory that the desire to destroy is itself a creative desire but, paradoxically, they wished to realize themselves in the very society which they opposed. Their anarchistic tendencies can be interpreted as a kind of rebellion against bourgeois regimentation and order. The Dadaists wanted the totally different, the opposite of everything the majority wanted. This also explains their predilection for scandal, noise, and subversion.

If we take a close look at Eggeling's abstract films and Schad's lenseless photos (Schadographs), Arp's abstract wood reliefs and Ball's sound-poems, Tzara's chaotic lyrics, and Janco's masks, it becomes obvious that Dada is not an art style but "a mental attitude" (Max Ernst), "a spiritual conviction" (Huelsenbeck, "Dadaist Manifesto," Berlin, 1918), a "life-style" (Huelsenbeck).

Part of the Dada program involved doing away with all artistic intention, all middle-class art ideals, all aesthetic structure. Tzara talked about the "destruction of art by artistic means. . . . The beginning of Dada was not the beginning of art but of disgust" (bibl. 3). Provocative acts and manifestos were at the very core of Dada activity. "Dada shows its truth in action" (Tzara). "The Dadaist considers it necessary to fight against art because he has seen through its fraud as a moral safety valve" (Huelsenbeck, bibl. 2).

The aggressiveness of the Zurich group, according to Miklavž Prosenc (bibl. 13), and the Anarchist views of its members had a great deal to do with their situation as immigrants, as rebellious outsiders. It was the culmination of a development that began in the nineteenth century when art ceased to be the preserve of the ruling class. Such nineteenth-century authors and artists as Flaubert and Baudelaire, Ensor and Van Gogh felt excluded and neglected by a society of which they considered themselves members. With every new avant-gardist trend in art, the chances of communication between art and public were further reduced, especially as the new works of art progressively lost their original aesthetic function, which was to give pleasure and thus affirm the existing order. More and more, the artist became a member of the opposition, a revolutionary. By the beginning of the twentieth century, he was deliberately placing himself outside society and had begun to attack it, sometimes singly, more often in groups. From this new position, the artist challenged middle-class standards. The proto-Dadaist Arthur Cravan wrote: "Every great artist has a knack for provocation."

Zurich Dada embodied this rebellious position of the twentieth-century avant-garde artist who, in Bakunin's spirit, desires the "unconditional destruction of all middle-class elements of culture" (Hugo Ball), but without so clear a political aim as the proletarian revolution. "Everything shall live, but one thing must disappear—the middle-class, fat-bellied, self-satisfied stuffed pig of spirituality, the guardian of all that is miserable" (Huelsenbeck, in *Neue Jugend*, 1917).

When World War I ended, eliminating the need for a common platform in exile, the Zurich Dada group dissolved. It had become apparent that the complete negation of all values and standards could not be made into an institution. In 1919, Arp, Janco, and Eggeling published a manifesto in which they announced their intention to participate in the state and its culture. It marked the end of the purely negative phase of Dada.

Ball had withdrawn from the group in 1917. By 1919 there was no longer any need to remain in exile. Arp returned to Cologne; Picabia, who had been in Zurich for a short time only, went to Paris. Soon, Janco and Tzara also showed up in Paris, while Eggeling and Richter settled in Berlin. There was no more Zurich Dada.

BERLIN

Huelsenbeck had gone in 1917 to Berlin, where—with Raoul Hausmann, John Heartfield, Wieland Herzfelde, George Grosz, Walter Mehring, and Erwin Piscator—he immediately set about reviving the Dada idea by means of lectures and manifestos. Other members of Berlin Dada were Johannes Baader, Hannah Höch, and Franz Jung. In 1918, they founded a Club Dada, published a large number of periodicals (most of them short-lived), arranged lectures and performances, and issued manifestos. The high point of their activities was the First International Dada Fair at the Dr. Otto Burchard gallery in 1920. The catalogue title page by Heartfield shows the specific aims of the Berlin Dadaists. "Dadaist man is the radical opponent of exploitation," says one superscription. "The Dada movement leads to the abolition of the art business," says another. Berlin in 1918 was very different from Zurich in 1916; the aims and activities of Dada were different in the two cities. In Zurich the war, war hysteria, and life in exile had been the determining factors; in the Berlin of 1918–19 revolution was in the air, against the kind of society that had caused the war. A general sense of uprising, of new beginnings, prevailed. The revolutionary situation appealed to the political and social consciousness of many intellectuals and artists who felt impelled to take sides. The Spartacists—a militant Socialist group—inflamed the minds of many artists and thinkers.

"Berlin Dada was politically oriented from the start. Thus, Dada was against all inwardness, against Expressionism—against abstract art, against all art as such" (Huelsenbeck, in *Dada siegt*, Berlin, 1920). Somewhat later, George Grosz wrote: "The movement I had joined influenced me so strongly that I considered all art senseless that did not present itself as a weapon for the political struggle" (bibl. 5).

Generally, Dada was inspired by the same revolutionary élan that had led to the founding of the Berlin Workers' Council for the Arts and the (initially equally political) Novembergruppe, with its branches in many German cities.

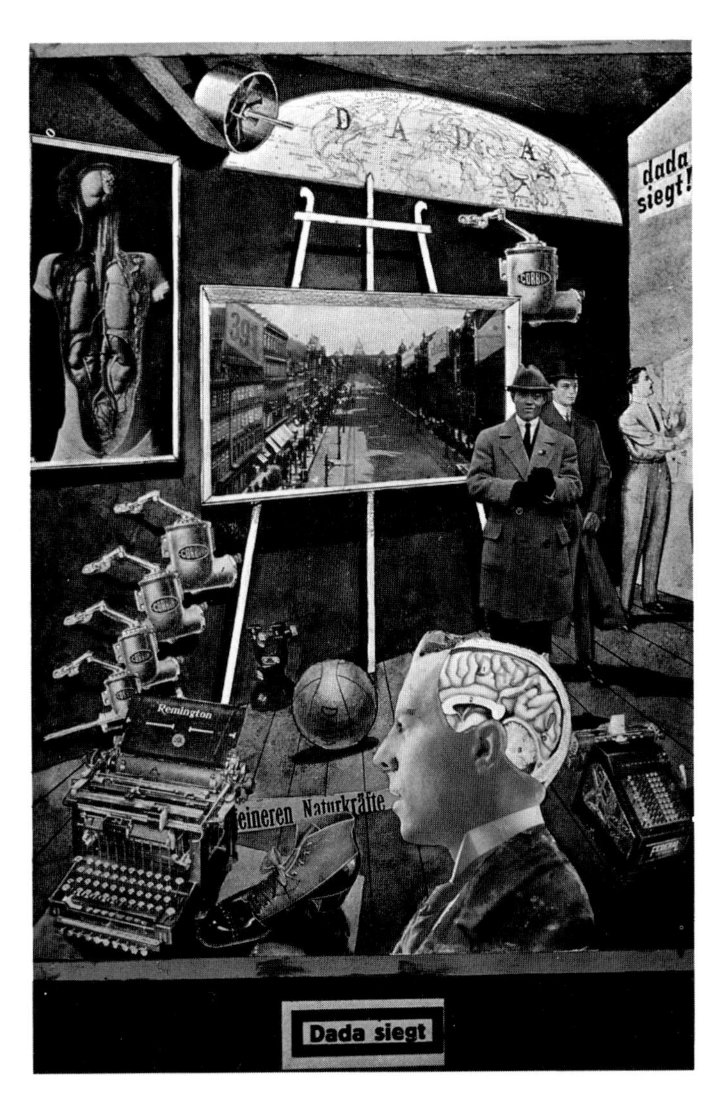

2. Raoul Hausmann. *Dada Is Victorious.* 1920. Collage

Wherever this élan remained a matter of pure ideals, it quickly faded away. Where it was based on a definite political idea, it led away from Dada; socio-political programs and membership in a political party—the Communist Party—were contrary to Dada's principle of total negation. Consequently, Huelsenbeck, who at first had declared that "Dada is German Bolshevism" (bibl. 2)—his idea of Bolshevism having been a general rebellion against middle-class society rather than anything as definite as the proletarian revolution—turned away from the radicals. Heartfield, on the other hand, gave himself completely to politics, producing photomontages with a radical political message; and Herzfelde brought out mainly left-wing literature in his publishing house. When the November Revolution lost its momentum and was finally squashed, and reactionary forces made their presence felt, many artists no longer considered a simple rejection of middle-class values sufficient. They placed their talents at the service of the Communist Party, in the hope that a new society could be built on the strength of the proletariat. By the end of 1921, Berlin Dada had ceased to exist.

COLOGNE

When Arp arrived in Cologne in 1919, he found two kindred spirits in Johannes T. Baargeld and Max Ernst. Together they founded the Dada group W/3 which in the course of the next few years became notorious for its polemical periodicals, spectacular exhibitions, and the disruption of a theatrical performance. *Dada-Vorfrühling* (Dada Spring's Awakening) was the name of an exhibition held in the courtyard of the Brauhaus Winter in 1920. Its goal was to shock the solid citizens of Cologne with provocative objects. The goal was met: "Works that had been destroyed by an infuriated public were constantly being replaced by new ones. Complaints (about fraud, pornography, public nuisance, etc.) were dismissed after the accused men had been questioned by the police. The exhibition was closed by order of the police" (Ernst, in bibl. 93). It reopened with a poster declaring, "Dada is for Peace and Order."

In Cologne, Dada was a special mixture of Baargeld's left-wing activism and Max Ernst's rebellion against the sanctimonious attitudes of the older generation and against middle-class provincialism. In Cologne, Dada was much more of an aesthetic rebellion than elsewhere, thanks, chiefly, to Max Ernst. Works of art were again being produced, though it was art that went "beyond painting" (Max Ernst). Arp soon left for Paris, and Ernst followed him in 1922. While still in Germany, Ernst had become friends with Breton, Tzara, and Eluard. Cologne Dada ended in 1921.

Meanwhile, in Hanover Kurt Schwitters produced his own kind of Dada, which was even more single-mindedly art-oriented than that of Cologne Dada. Huelsenbeck reported later: "We called him an abstract Spitzweg, a Caspar David Friedrich of the Dada revolution" (in bibl. 7).

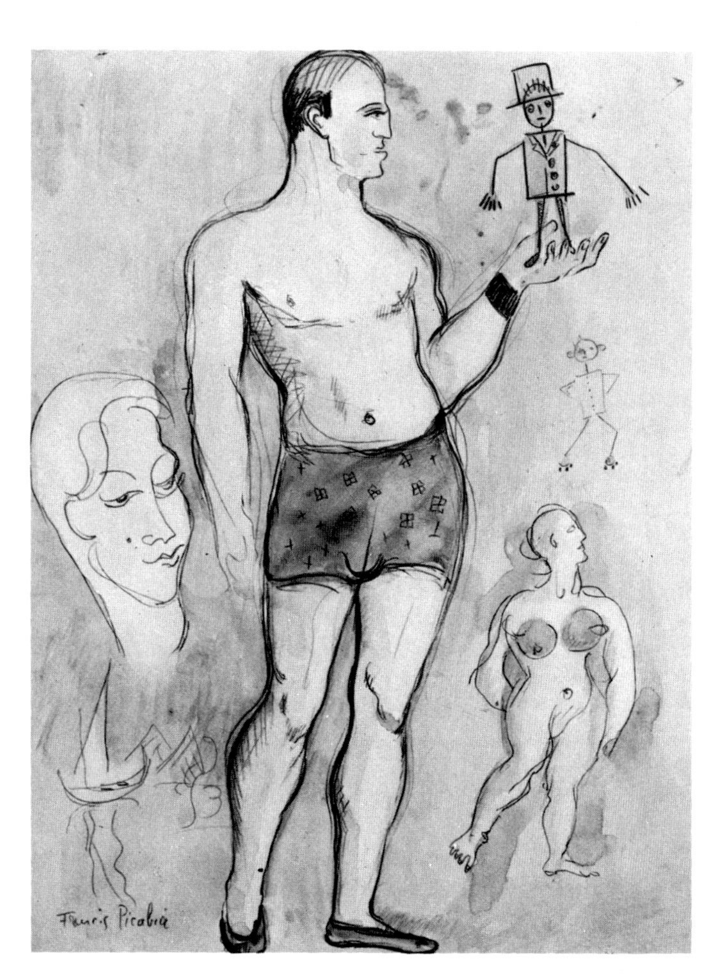

3. Francis Picabia. *Probable Portrait of Arthur Cravan.* 1925

PARIS

Huelsenbeck had carried the Dada idea to Berlin, Arp had taken it to Cologne. When Picabia and Tzara moved from Zurich to Paris about 1920, and were joined there by Marcel Duchamp, Man Ray and, somewhat later, by Arp and Ernst, Dada blossomed once more—and once again in an entirely different atmosphere. The ground had been prepared by Guillaume Apollinaire and Louis Aragon, André Breton, and Philippe Soupault, who had started an authoritative periodical, *Littérature*, in 1919. Soon, other publications began to appear, most notably Picabia's *391*. Due to Tzara's influence, literary activities predominated in Paris. In 1920–21 many spectacular events were staged. Once, on February 5, 1920, thirty-eight speakers read (often simultaneously) various Dada manifestos. A year later, a series of absurd excursions—soon to be discontinued—to historic sites were arranged. A mock trial of the reactionary novelist Maurice Barrés created a schism in the movement. Tzara and Picabia wanted, each in his own way, the dissolution of society, while Breton's aim was to change society and to activate the human unconscious in a systematic way: "Let it not be said that Dada served any other purpose than to keep us in this open, wide-awake state in which we find ourselves—and from which we shall now quite deliberately remove ourselves in order to turn toward that which calls us" (Breton in *Littérature*, 4, 1922). During a performance of Tzara's *Coeur à gaz*, in 1923, there was a fist fight between Anarchist Dadaists and those who later became Surrealists and who were seeking new ideas. A certain power struggle, or a struggle for leadership, may have played its part in that fight, with Breton and Tzara the chief contenders.

In contrast to the Zurich, Berlin, and Cologne versions of Dada, the Paris group with Aragon, Breton, Eluard, Péret, Picabia, Georges Ribemont-Dessaignes, Soupault, and Tzara was a group movement of a literary avant-garde. It was an intellectual branch of the artistic opposition. Its antecedents were the publications of Apollinaire and Pierre Reverdy and their followers. Shocking the public, establishing a generation gap, or taking political action were not the main goals of these artists. What they wanted most of all was to establish and proclaim a literary avant-garde in truly French tradition, to be the successors of Rimbaud, Lautréamont, Jarry. Visual art seemed less important to this

4. Catalogue for the First International Dada Fair (title page with typography by John Heartfield), Berlin, 1920

part of the movement, but it was to be of enormous importance for Surrealism.

Dada would be unthinkable without the chaotic manifestations of the Italian Futurists or without Duchamp's provocative contributions, the Readymades, to various major exhibitions; these were everyday utensils (a bottle-drying rack, a urinal, a snow shovel) rather than works of art, and they established the principle of artless art. Of equal importance for the Surrealist movement were Picabia's works and his attitude toward life (he deemed life more important than art, which he considered only a shadow of his adventures) and Arthur Cravan's pre-Dada nonsense activities.

Dada's massive protest against middle-class aesthetics consisted of the abandonment of painting and sculpture, the creation of new forms of art, and the development of a kind of art that does not produce any objects. These Dada "actions" were similar to the Happenings of the 1960s. Hans Richter has grasped the Dada paradox: "Dada hates art, but Dada renews art by means of an 'artistic antiart movement.' "

Duchamp produced the first Readymades and also—with his *Apolinère Enameled* (fig. 11)—the modified Readymade, which Max Ernst independently evolved at the same time. The sound-poems and optophonetic (rebus) poems that were written in Zurich and Berlin were forerunners of Phonetic and Visual Poetry. Independently of each other, both Ball and Hausmann developed early forms of Concrete Poetry. Noise "music" was being composed. Christian Schad invented Schadographs, Man Ray worked out his Rayographs and aerographs. In Berlin and Cologne, artists produced photocollages which, systematically developed, became photomontages. Schwitters created his *Merzbau*—a kind of environment. Picabia and Max Ernst discovered the uses of trivial illustrative material. In almost every Dada

5. Kurt Schwitters. *The "And" Picture.* 1919. Collage

effect. Contrary to Dada's actual intentions, it not only demolished traditional art, it also established a base for new approaches which Dada itself did not explore. In this respect, Dada was not an art style: it was a protest that extended to all forms of art and included life as well; it was a "cleansing process," an attitude toward existing things, on which the Surrealists were able to build.

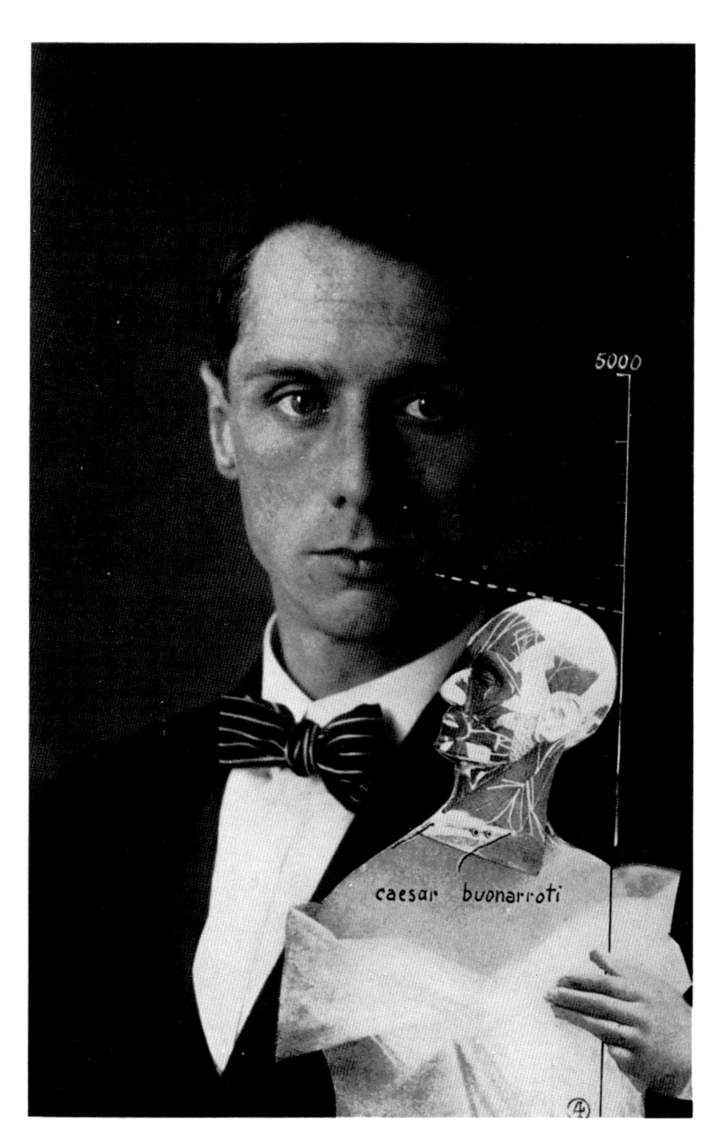

6. Max Ernst. *Self-Portrait.* 1920. Photocollage

7. Max Ernst. *Trophy Hypertrophied.* 1919. Technical engraving altered with ink

center, typography received totally new impulses. Max Ernst took the Cubist technique of *papier collé* and turned it into collage. Arp and Ernst collaborated on certain collages they called Fatagaga. Arp accepted the accidental as an element of his art. Eggeling and Richter infused avant-garde photography with new life, first with abstract stills and then with abstract motion pictures.

By renouncing the artistic transformation of reality and matter, by approving new working methods and preferring artlessness in art, Dada erased the boundaries between art-reality and life-reality (for instance, when chance and accident were accepted as picture elements) as well as the boundaries between the various categories of art. In this respect, Dada went beyond Cubism and Futurism. With all the rage and protest against convention, Dada had a realistic, rational attitude toward reality and toward the art scene. For this reason its call for total destruction, its questioning of all categories, standards, and values had a fruitful

8. Jean Arp. *La Trousse d'un Da.* 1920

9. Max Ernst. *Ice Landscapes.* 1920. Modified Readymade

Proto-Surrealism—"Disquieting Dream Reality"

"In times of great uncertainty about our mission," wrote André Breton, the head of the Surrealist movement, "we often looked at the fixed points of Lautréamont and De Chirico, which sufficed to determine our straight line" (*Le Surréalisme et la peinture*, 1928).

Giorgio de Chirico, whom the Surrealists initially accepted with such enthusiasm, had been hailed in 1914 by Apollinaire as "the most amazing painter of our time." Although he never actually belonged to the Surrealist movement, De Chirico participated in the first big Surrealist exhibition in the Galerie Pierre in Paris (1925). Breton and Eluard had bought some of his canvases in the early twenties. Max Ernst, René Magritte, and Yves Tanguy are all greatly indebted to him. From 1924 to 1929, the most important Surrealist publication, *La Révolution surréaliste*, often reproduced his works, even though, after 1918, his style had taken a turn toward classicism, to which the Surrealists objected. The *Dictionnaire abrégé du surréalisme*, published in 1938, simply says: "The work of this artist which inspired Surrealism ended in 1918." Still, it is generally conceded that Surrealism owes a great deal to De Chirico.

De Chirico produced his most important works between 1911 and 1918. Unlike the Italian Futurists who were his contemporaries, he was motivated neither by a need to break away from tradition nor by a fascination with modern urban life. De Chirico's inspiration was based on secondary experiences: an encounter with the paintings of Arnold Böcklin and the writing of Nietzsche. Up until 1910, his paintings resembled those of Böcklin, but this is not as important, in view of his later development, as are his comments on Böcklin's work. In an essay of 1930, De Chirico wrote: "Böcklin's metaphysical power derives from precision, from the clear definition of objects. He never painted diffusely. He never drew an inaccurate outline. That is what constitutes his classicism and his greatness. . . . Every one of his works produces the same kind of shock, the kind of uneasy surprise we all feel when we meet a stranger whom we think we have seen before, though we don't know where or when." In Böcklin's work the fact that the real can appear unreal and the unreal can seem real, that banal subjects can contain fantastic components, fascinated De Chirico. As for Nietzsche, De Chirico wrote in his autobiography of 1945 that what he found most interesting in the philosopher-writer was "a strange, dark poetry, infinitely mysterious and lonely, based on *atmosphere* . . . on the atmosphere of an afternoon in autumn when the weather is clear and the shadows are longer than they have been all summer, because the sun stands low in the sky." And he added, "The place where this phenomenon can best be observed is the Italian city of Turin."

Whereas Böcklin tended to stress the fantastic aura of reality, Nietzsche attempted to make the objective world translucent. These concepts determined the work of De

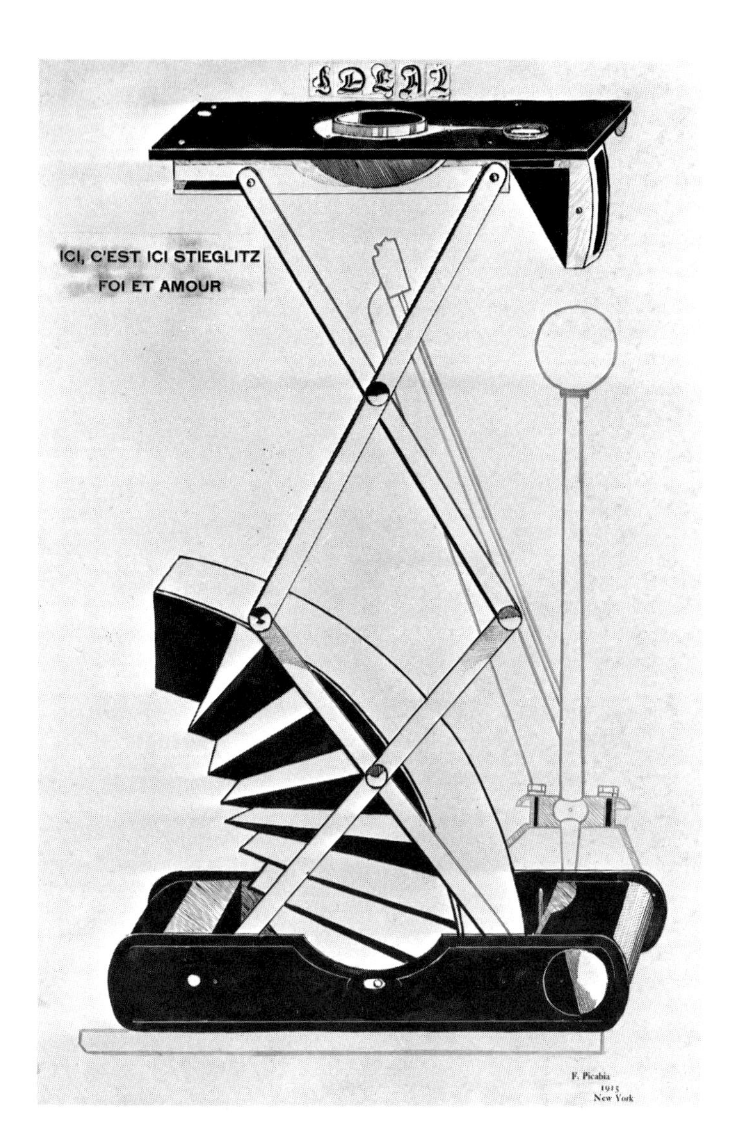

10. Francis Picabia. *Ici, c'est içi Stieglitz.* 1915. Pen and red and black ink

11. Marcel Duchamp. *Apolinère Enameled.* 1916–17. Modified Readymade

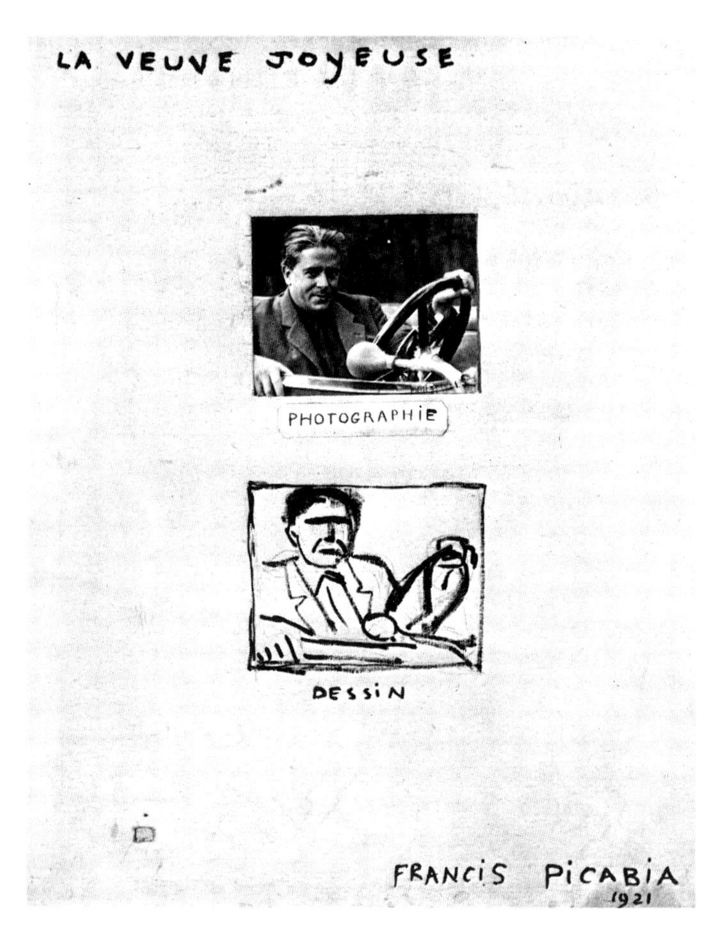

12. Francis Picabia. *The Merry Widow* (*Self-Portrait*). 1921

Chirico. He was stirred by Nietzsche's description of Turin's city squares. In 1911, he visited the city and saw those squares: they became one of his most important pictorial subjects.

The German Symbolist artist Max Klinger was another important influence. In 1920, De Chirico wrote: "Psychologically more complex, but less classical than Böcklin, Klinger creates an extremely disquieting dream reality, by combining in a single composition scenes of contemporary life and visions of Antiquity."

The same aspects that fascinated De Chirico in the work of Böcklin and Nietzsche also excited the Surrealists: the dream reality, the disquieting atmosphere, the combination of the real and the unreal. In 1911—the year he came to Paris and began work on his "metaphysical" pictures (so described by Apollinaire)—De Chirico painted the following inscription on a self-portrait: *"Et quid amabo nisi quod aenigma est?"* (And what shall I love if not an enigma?). Enigma is precisely what fascinated the Surrealists.

In illusionist art, which ran counter to the developments of the time, Cubism and de Stijl, the logic of Renaissance painting was converted into a kind of antilogic which the

Surrealists found terrifying and therefore desirable. They recognized De Chirico as their immediate predecessor, a proto-Surrealist. The mysterious way in which he placed disparate objects side by side, transformed human beings into objects, puzzlingly applied conflicting angles of perspective, and generally created pictures whose effect was completely unreal while all the elements in them were painted with complete realism—all this profoundly impressed the Surrealists. His influence can be observed especially in the works of Max Ernst, Salvador Dali, and Yves Tanguy.

MAX ERNST

Max Ernst first saw De Chirico's paintings reproduced in the Italian periodical *Valori plastici*, in Munich in 1919. He reacted to this encounter by producing a portfolio of lithographs called *Fiat modes* (1919), which he declared to be an homage to De Chirico. The ingredients of these pictures indicate how profoundly Ernst had been impressed by De Chirico's conflicting angles of perspective and his dressmaker dummies.

At the time, Ernst was living in Cologne, where he worked out a whole series of new techniques, while keeping in close touch with some of the Paris Dadaists. He made automatic drawings—combination prints, worked over with pen or brush. He made rubbings of large wooden letters, an early form of *frottage*. He created modified Readymades from illustrations in scientific catalogues, advertisements, and textbooks. He produced works from various kinds of materials (fig. 9), and, somewhat later, used late-nineteenth-century engravings for the same purpose. He also produced photocollages, some of which were published in small editions.

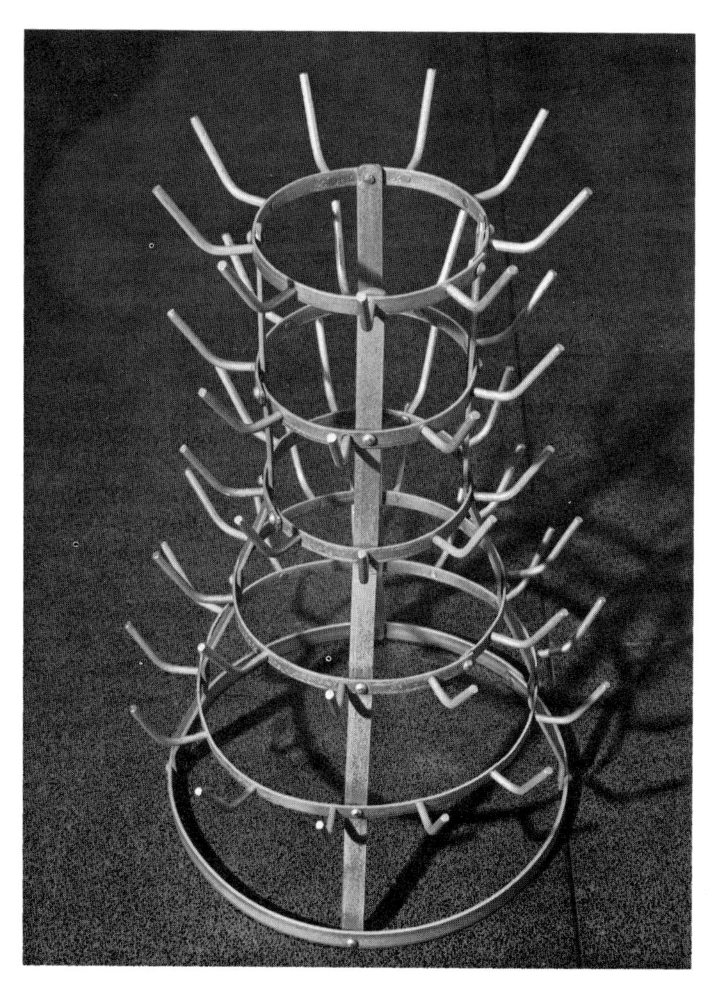

13. Marcel Duchamp. *Bottlerack*. 1914. Readymade

The principle underlying all of this work is collage. Ernst has defined the collage technique as the "systematic exploitation of an accidental or deliberate meeting of two unrelated realities on a plane that is related to neither—and the spark of poetry that is kindled by the coming together of these realities" (bibl. 93).

The *papier collé* technique which the French Cubists had developed was based on formal unity. The Dada collage is based on the incongruity of the various picture elements.

We find the principle of collage exemplified by De Chirico's pictures, although no cutting and pasting took place in their execution. Breton's reference to Lautréamont and De Chirico as the two fixed points of Surrealism (quoted above) confirms this affinity for the collage principle, for it was Lautréamont who coined the now famous phrase about the beauty of the accidental encounter of a sewing machine and an umbrella on a dissecting table. "When the strangest things come together through a place, a time, a peculiar resemblance, the results are amazing units and curious connections." This quotation from the German Romantic poet Novalis anticipates Max Ernst's definition of collage. It may, incidentally, suggest the reason why the Surrealists also considered the Romantics forerunners of the movement. In De Chirico's work, the combination of unrelated objects appears as an application of the montage principle, a principle that had been in existence for some time, and which Max Klinger, too, had applied from time to time. This principle was to become one of the trademarks of Surrealism. The collage principle redefined the very idea of artistic activity. The creative process itself had become more important than its end result; that process consisted of the selection of one or more already existing subjects and of their alteration, which integrated them into the realm of art. The artist's work was reduced to the act of combining and modifying various elements of reality. The interaction between a found object and the artist who modified it permitted accident to play an important part. But such accidents could also be produced deliberately and thus controlled—as Max Ernst has pointed out. In his work and also in Hans Arp's, accident is not nearly as prevalent as is deliberate design.

Thus, Max Ernst's collages—developed about 1920—which were based on consciously controlled accident clearly show one of the leading principles of Surrealism: incongruous combination. To understand Surrealism, we must keep in mind that the principle of incongruous combination is not a stylistic device but a method for making pictures.

No doubt, the Paris Dadaists were greatly impressed by

the modified Readymades and by the collages made from old woodcuts or modern advertisements, which Ernst used to satirize the older generation. He showed them in the 1920 exhibition called *Beyond Painting* at the Galerie Au Sans Pareil. They have played an important role in the development of Surrealist techniques. But what impressed the Paris group—and especially Eluard—even more were Ernst's large pictures, painted between 1921 and 1924, just before Surrealism was officially proclaimed (colorplates 4 and 5). These pictures, with their Verism of the Improbable, anticipate Surrealism. Ernst used De Chirico's paintings for his model and created picture stages of fictitious realism whose ultimate effect (calculated, no doubt) gave them the appearance of materialized dreams. He also borrowed a figure from De Chirico's *The Child's Brain* (1914; fig. 14) for his own *Pietà or Revolution by Night* (1923; fig. 15), which hints at a father-and-son conflict.

Max Ernst had broken with Dada by that time. He was painting pictures again, which meant that he was striving to create pictorial unity, fractured though it might be. The deliberate combination of incongruous elements was carried over from his collages to his paintings.

Having taken an intense interest in psychological problems, Ernst had studied the writing of Sigmund Freud. His own childhood obsessions show up in his paintings, of course, but unlike De Chirico's they did not get there unconsciously. Instead, Ernst points them up in his paintings, picture-book fashion. This was especially appreciated by those Paris Dadaists who had just begun to sever their own connections with the group. Ernst had learned from De Chirico and from Freud that incongruous combination and verism are two methods by which conscious logic can be replaced by dream logic.

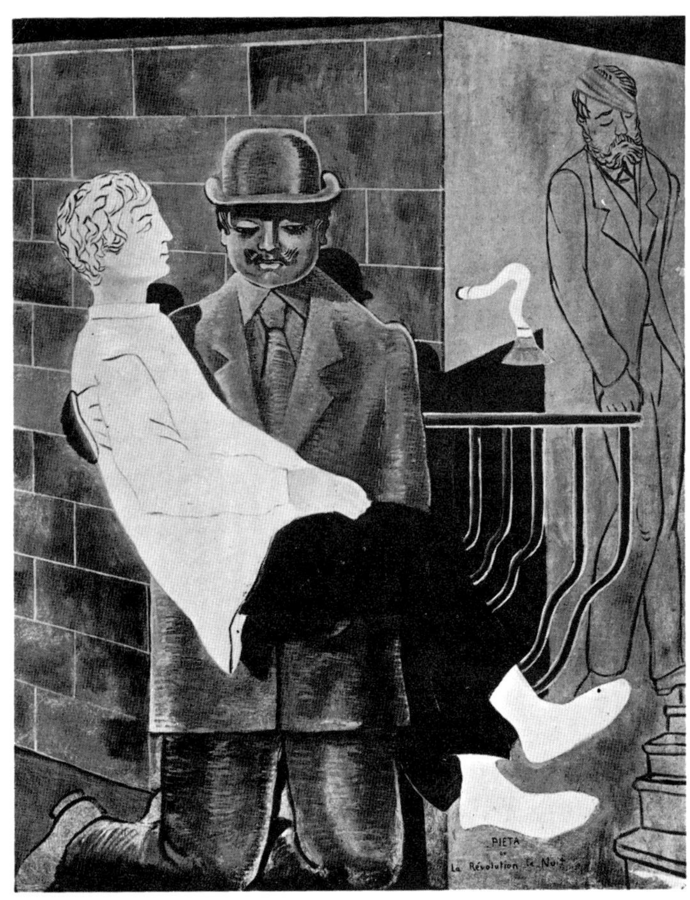

15. Max Ernst. *Pietà or Revolution by Night.* 1923. Oil on canvas

14. Giorgio de Chirico. *The Child's Brain.* 1914. Oil on canvas

Breton's 1924 Manifesto

In 1916, André Breton, then an assistant physician, met Jacques Vaché, a patient in the neurological division of the hospital in Nantes. Vaché, who engaged in nonsense actions and was a fervent admirer of Alfred Jarry, practiced the kind of alienation from middle-class life-styles to which the Dadaists aspired. He became an idol of the Surrealists, especially after his suicide in 1919.

Somewhat later, Breton conducted his first experiments with the insane at the psychiatric center in Saint-Dizier. He drew pictures of their dreams and committed their free associations to paper in order to analyze the patients by

Freudian methods. In 1919, he published a slim volume, *Les Chants magnétiques*, consisting of texts he had developed together with Philippe Soupault by the free-association method, that is, automatically.

The antibourgeois impetus of Vaché and a preoccupation with irrational mental processes dominate André Breton's subsequent theoretical writing. Breton had been a member of the Paris group of Dada, but he had gradually moved away from it. In 1924, he published his first Surrealist manifesto, which proclaimed a new movement.

The first time the word *Surrealist* appeared was in a program for a Diaghilev ballet. The ballet was *Parade*, with music by Erik Satie, decor and costumes by Picasso, and choreography by Léonide Massine. The program notes were by Apollinaire. Later, in 1917, Apollinaire used the word again, in the subtitle of his drama *Les Mamelles de Tirésias*—"a Surrealist drama." In an essay written in 1922, Breton said, "Up to a certain point one knows what my friends and I mean by Surrealism. This word, which is not our invention and which we could have retained as an extremely vague, questionable designation, is used by us in a perfectly precise sense. We use it to describe a certain psychic automatism that comes very close to dream, a state that is very hard to circumscribe today" (*Les Pas perdus*, 1924).

This general declaration, in which the key words are "psychic automatism" and "dream state," was followed by a period of automatic writing whose main practitioners were Aragon, Crevel, Desnos, and Péret. And this, in turn, resulted in a new theoretical definition, lexicon-style, which we find in the first manifesto:

> *Surrealism*. Noun, masc. Pure psychic automatism by which one tries to express verbally, in writing, or by any other method, the actual process of thinking. Thought-dictation without any control exercised by reason, beyond any aesthetic or ethical consideration.
>
> Encyclopedia. Philosophy. Surrealism is based on the belief in the superior reality of certain heretofore neglected forms of associations, in the omnipotence of the dream, in the free-wheeling play of thought. It wants to bring about the ultimate destruction of all other psychic mechanisms and put itself in their place in order to solve the primary problems of life.

Here is a manifesto—always a favorite form of communication for avant-garde movements—that is by no means as poetic or provocative as the Dada manifestos. In an apparent effort to achieve a kind of scientific accuracy, it describes, in theory, a goal of Surrealism that has nothing whatever to do with Dada.

This new goal is the systematic exploitation and study of general, unconscious qualities. According to Freud, certain events in one's life can vanish for a while, or for always, from one's consciousness; they are repressed, relegated to the unconscious. Repression is caused by taboos, first of all. Freud had shown that the unconscious was real and that it had an enormous influence on everything we do. His psychoanalytical method is a way of making the unconscious conscious, of observing its mechanisms and laws, its manifestations in dreams and in "slips." The Surrealists' belief in the "superior reality of certain, previously neglected forms of association, in the omnipotence of the dream" (Breton) is, in the Freudian sense, simply a belief in the unconscious as the original and only true creative force.

Breton's somewhat forced and peremptory definition at the outset of the manifesto is explained and modified further on. He declares that the reign of rationalism, of civilization and progress, with their compulsive utilitarianism, has suppressed certain essential human powers, especially the power of imagination. In his view, automatic writing is a means toward liberating the unconscious and restoring man's total potential. No doubt Peter Bürger is right when he says that Surrealism did not try to establish a new literary technique, but tried to eliminate literature altogether, not in order to destroy it but in order to do away with the division between art and life (bibl. 48).

Breton's declaration that the unconscious alone is relevant, incidentally, is contradicted or, at least, given limits in the manifesto itself. A few pages prior to the above-quoted

16. Max Ernst. Woodcut-collage from *Une Semaine de bonté*. 1934

statement, Breton wrote: "Perhaps imagination is about to recover its ancient rights. If there are mysterious powers hidden in the depth of our mind, capable of strengthening or defeating those at the surface, then we have every reason to capture them; first to capture them and then, if necessary, to subject them to control by reason." These remarks clearly contradict the rigorous rejection of "control through reason" stipulated elsewhere in the manifesto. Indeed, the antirational tendency of the manifesto is scarcely borne out by Surrealist practice, except for the period of widespread experimentation with automatic writing. Thus it is not at all surprising to find Aragon writing in 1928 that "Surrealism is inspiration—realized, recognized, accepted and then utilized" ("Traité du style"). This statement, which Aragon must have based on his own observation of poetic and literary methods, puts the emphasis clearly on the conscious *recognition* of the unconscious.

In his analysis of the first Surrealist manifesto, Hans Holländer has pointed out that Surrealist techniques are by no means irrational (bibl. 46). In his first version of the manifesto, Breton mentioned a thirteenth-century scholar, Raymond Lully, as an ancestor of Surrealism. Lully developed a system of combining divergent elements whose subsequent practitioners include Jonathan Swift, Athanasius Kircher, Leibnitz, Novalis, Mallarmé, and, as quoted by Breton, Pierre Reverdy and, finally, Max Ernst. According to Lully, a mechanical system of combination can be used to prove and unite all things, even those that are totally contradictory. Of course, this kind of incongruous combination can bring about absurd entities that make a new statement with, occasionally, electrifying effect. In other words, the *results* of this incongruous combination—which had been used in collage quite a while before the Surrealist manifesto appeared—may be irrational, but the application of the method is perfectly rational. In this respect, Surrealism is able to control its methods, but not its results.

Thus, while there is no stylistic unity to be found in the works of the Surrealists, there is this one unifying characteristic: incongruous combination. With the artist's full awareness of the psychoanalytical meaning of certain picture elements, these elements are brought together in ways that produce unexpected effects.

Frottage, which Max Ernst developed in 1925, after being influenced by Breton's manifesto, is a derivative of this principle. It is based on metamorphosis. Tools and method are consciously chosen; the result, produced with full command of the creative process, can be surprising. The simple and familiar is turned into something unknown and unfathomable by the method of metamorphosis and incongruous combination.

"The most important new tool is the moment of surprise. The surprise element and the importance ascribed to baffling effects make this new trend different from all that went before in art and literature." These words by Apollinaire were written in 1917 (in *Esprit nouveau*). No wonder the Surrealists revered him. Surprise, ambiguity, and the unknown are considered enriching stimulants. They open up new possibilities by restoring the total human potential. Surprise has the character of inspiration. This is what the Surrealists sought and this is what Breton essentially demanded in his first manifesto.

17. Pablo Picasso. *Portrait of André Breton, Three-Quarter View.* 1923. Drypoint

Activities and Disagreements, 1924–1929

In 1922, the Dadaists prevented Breton from organizing a "Congress to establish guidelines and defend the Modern Spirit" in Paris. Thereupon Breton, Aragon, Eluard, and Péret broke with Dada. The circle around Tristan Tzara wished to remain in a state of Anarchism. The circle around André Breton felt a need for new objectives. The Surrealist manifesto of 1924 proves that these objectives were not directly related to the anti-aesthetic ideas of Dada. Although Surrealism harked back to Rimbaud, Lautréamont, and Jarry—a very definitely French avant-garde tradition—

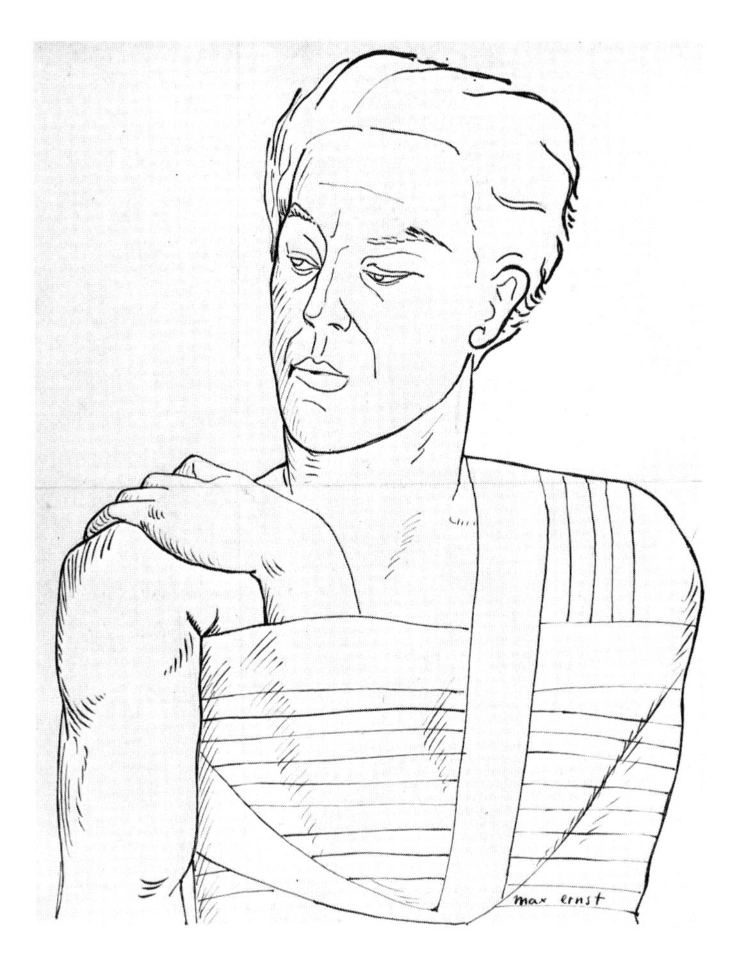

18. Max Ernst. *Portrait of André Breton.* 1924. Ink

and was based on Dada rebellion, it still must be regarded as a road to new knowledge, directed toward previously neglected facets of human existence: the miraculous, the surprising, insanity, dream, the unconscious, and hallucination. In his manifesto, Breton listed the names of those who had sworn to his program: Aragon, Crevel, Desnos, Eluard, Georges Malkine, Max Morise, Pierre Naville, Péret, Soupault, Roger Vitrac, and others. They are all writers. Picabia, in the final issue of his magazine, *391*, in 1924, staged an all-out attack on the Surrealists. That same year, Eluard tried to emulate Rimbaud by running away from civilization; suddenly disappearing from Paris, he later reemerged in Saigon, where he and Ernst met. But this attempt to reenact an experience that had become enshrined in literature was as fruitless as was Eckermann's effort to relive Goethe's experiences in Italy. The year 1924 also saw the publication of Aragon's *Une Vague de rêves*, a résumé of Surrealist art, especially in the field of automatic writing.

Some painters and sculptors were represented in the magazine *La Révolution surréaliste,* which began publication in 1924. Originally produced by Naville and Péret, the magazine was taken over by Breton in 1929. In contrast to Dada magazines, which were typographically attractive, though chaotic in content, *La Révolution surréaliste* was sober in appearance. Naville wanted to make it look as much as possible like an immensely popular natural-history magazine of the period, *La Nature*.

In the introduction to the first issue of *La Révolution surréaliste,* Boiffard, Eluard, and Vitrac demanded that every family should report its dreams at breakfast. The issue contains dream reports by De Chirico, Breton, and René Gauthier, and numerous automatic texts by Surrealists. Reverdy contributed an article on the value of dreams: "Dreaming and thinking are two different aspects of the same ability; its front and rear view." Aragon discussed the importance of humor in poetry in an article illustrated by a photograph from a Buster Keaton film. Aragon quoted Jarry's observation that humor is a form of *surréalité*. There is a photograph of a certain Germaine Berton, surrounded by photographs of all the Surrealists; the pictures include De Chirico, Max Ernst, Sigmund Freud, Man Ray, and Picasso. Germaine Berton was a young anarchist who had just shot and killed Marius Plateau, head of the right-wing group called Les Camelots du Roi, in the editorial office of a right-wing magazine. The illustrations of the first issue of *La Révolution surréaliste* are by Ernst, Masson, Man Ray, and Picasso.

Also in 1924, a Bureau de Recherches Surréalistes (Bureau of Surrealist Research) was established—without Eluard and Ernst, who were in Saigon. Aragon wrote: "In the

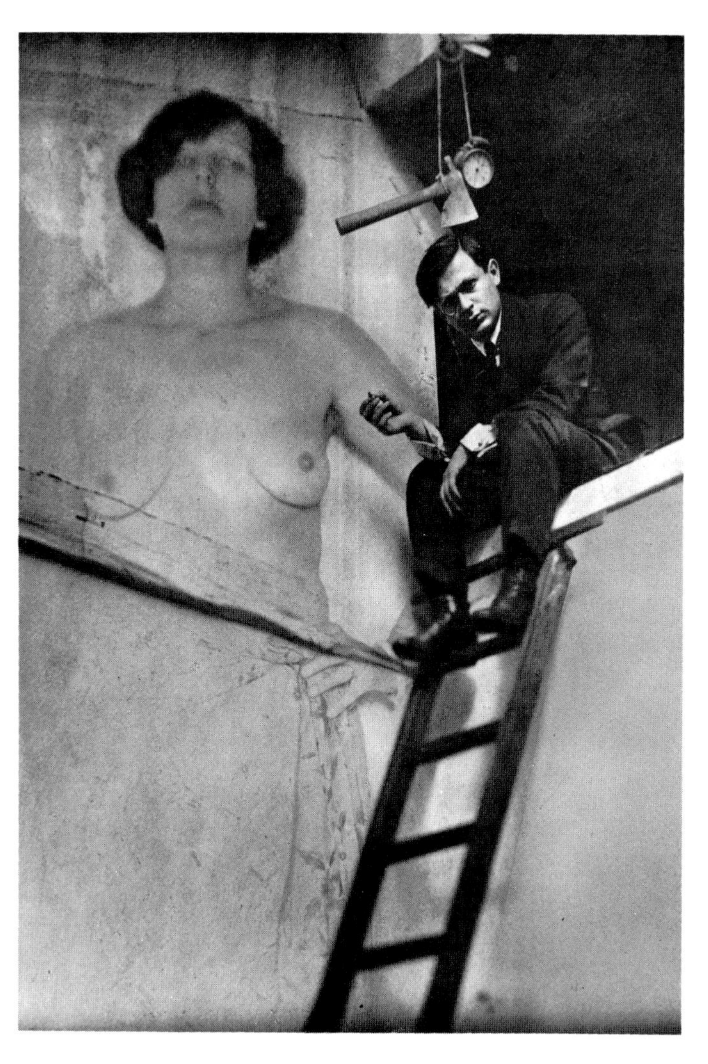

19. Man Ray. Photograph of Tristan Tzara. About 1921

20. André Masson. *André Breton.* 1941

21. Francis Picabia. *Paul Eluard.* 1920

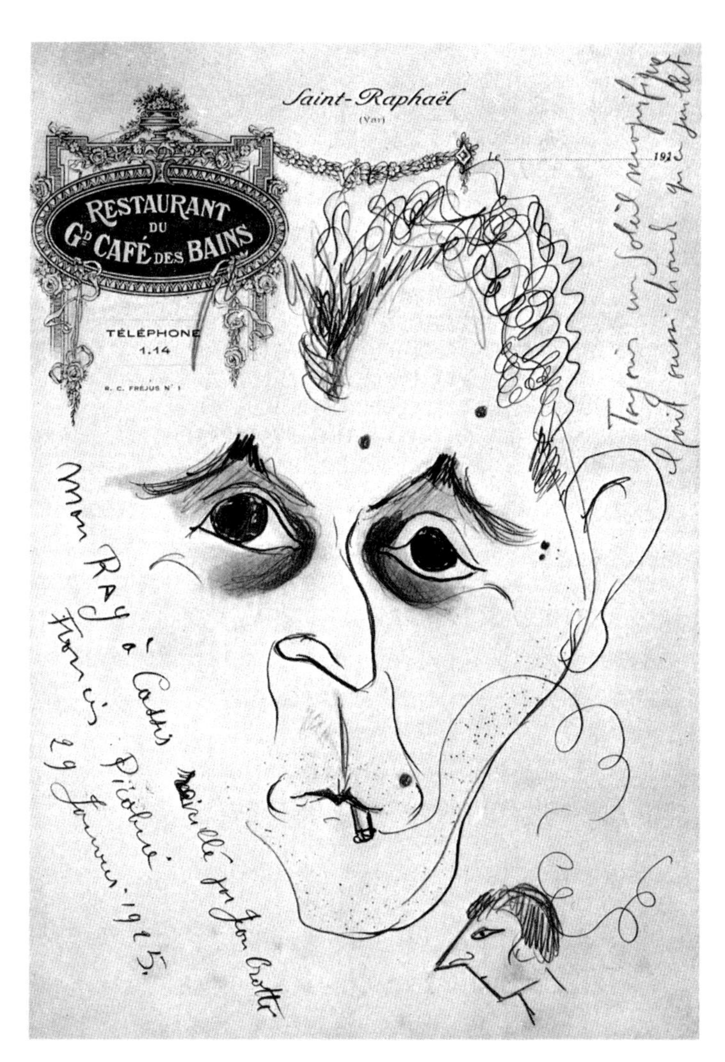

22. Francis Picabia. *Man Ray.* 1925

rue de Grenelle 15, we have furnished a romantic refuge for all those ideas that resist being categorized, and for all stubborn rebellions. Any hope left in this desperate world may turn its last ecstatic glance toward our humble abode: a new Declaration of the Rights of Man must somehow be launched, that is our goal" (*Une Vague de rêves,* 1924). Tremendous amounts of propaganda were to spread the ideas of Surrealism. A sensation was caused by an article entitled "Un Cadavre," in which the Surrealists severely criticized Anatole France, who had just died and whom they detested despite his socialist tendencies. Breton said: "When Anatole France left this earth, he at least took a little piece of the slave spirit along." And Aragon added: "The thought that he lived at all is enough to make you mad."

Breton's manifesto notwithstanding, the movement had no real program in that first year. What can be observed are its predilection for the dream, the destruction of middle-class morality, and a general desire to create something entirely different. There is a vague endeavor to make art and life identical, but there are no art-political or socio-political ideas to dominate the movement.

In this respect, the year 1925 brought several important changes. At first there was a disagreement with the pro-

Communist magazine *Clarté,* which was followed by a disagreement over the war in Morocco.

Like all Communists in the 1920s, the Communists in France took orders from the U.S.S.R. When Aragon made some remarks against "half-witted Moscow" in his contribution to "Un Cadavre," he was instantly attacked by *Clarté.* His reply, published in the same magazine, gives us a glimpse of the Surrealists' political attitude: "I would once more emphasize that the disgraceful revolutionary business that's been going on in Eastern Europe these last few years contributes nothing at all to the solution of the real problems of human existence. Anyone who still calls that sort of thing 'revolutionary' is doing violence to the language."

The title of the magazine *La Révolution surréaliste* must be understood in that same sense: it has nothing to do with political upheaval in favor of the suppressed masses. It is a Surrealist, a spiritual, an idealist "revolution." Maurice Nadeau, in his *History of Surrealism,* makes this clear: "The Surrealist Revolution first of all has no desire to change the objective, visible conditions of life by fair means or foul. What it wishes to do is to set in motion the thinking processes of all individuals. Thus, any Surrealist revolution aims at the innermost essence of man, at the realm of thought" (bibl. 39).

In a Declaration of January 27, 1925, we find this statement: "We are firmly resolved to bring about a revolution," but "we only joined the words 'surrealism' and 'revolution' so closely in order to show how unselfish the aims of this revolution are, how unworldly, how indifferent to material goods, indeed, how basically desperate and hopeless it is."

The artistic avant-garde, as represented in the twenties by the Surrealists, stood in opposition to the progressive politics of the day. It preferred inwardness to the active struggle for an improvement in social conditions. Despite its rebellious acts, this avant-garde confined its aims to the liberation of the individual, as set forth in its manifesto. It is a kind of retreat—realistic though it may have been—that one finds amazing for that particular period, especially when it is compared with the situation in Germany, where most artists took an intense and active interest in politics.

A pamphlet published in April 1925 by Artaud, Boiffard, Michel Leiris, Masson, and Naville shows that the arguments continued of whether precedence should be given to Surrealism or to revolution. "Before they [the undersigned] can decide whether to proceed in a revolutionary or a Surrealist manner, they must be filled with a certain kind of rage to begin with. They consider this rage the most suitable mood by which to attain what may be called Surrealist illumination. . . ." The pamphlet does not say what motivates this rage or against what it might be directed. One might regard this rage as the smallest common denominator of a group of people who wish to proceed together without having reached any definitive agreement about a common goal.

There was so much controversy at the time that even Breton, who had matters firmly in hand, did not dare give a straightforward answer to the question about the aims of Surrealism: "Is Surrealism purely a power of resistance, or is it a complex of theoretical ideas, or is it a system based on the mingling of all levels and realms, or is it the foundation of a new social order? No matter how this question is answered, everyone should try to get as much out of Surrealism as he can. In any case, we will not be deterred by internal contradictions" (*La Révolution surréaliste,* Vol. 4, 1925). "The one thing which the initial philosophy of Surrealism had in common with Lautréamont and Rimbaud, that united our destiny with theirs for all times, was our hatred of war" (*Qu'est-ce que le Surréalisme?,* 1934). As the Dadaists before them had been united by a war, so now the Surrealists were forced to make a joint political decision. The rebellion of Abd-el-Krim in the French colony of Morocco in 1925 resulted in an imperialist attack on the colonists by France. The members of the Académie Française and many other Frenchmen approved the suppression of the Moroccan independence movement. In a proclamation, the Académie Française pronounced, "The intellectuals are on the side of the fatherland." But the Surrealists sided with Abd-el-Krim, which brought them close to the Communist camp and to the authors of *Clarté.*

Thereupon, *La Révolution surréaliste* and *Clarté* tried to come to an agreement about future cooperation. They published a joint manifesto, "La Révolution d'abord et toujours," together with the staff and readership of two other magazines, *Philosophies* and *Correspondence.* This represented a turning point in the political stance of the Surrealists. For the first time, they involved themselves in Marxist arguments about the relation of economics to suppression: "For more than a hundred years, the dignity of man has been debased to a mere commodity. It is unfair and monstrous enough that the have-nots are subjugated by the haves; but when this subjugation goes beyond the framework of a simple wage relationship and takes on the dimensions of the kind of slavery in which the people are kept by the international bankers, then injustice has become so crass that not even a bloodbath could expunge it." The turnabout is now complete: "We are not Utopians; what interests us in this revolution are its social aspects."

It is easy to call this new position a mere attitude. But we must not underestimate the effect on the Surrealists of the brutal war against the Moroccans. We need only compare it with the effect of the Vietnam war on intellectuals the world over and their reaction to the imperialism of the United States. Breton was to say later that the war of 1925–26 had led to a "phase of critical debate" which made it necessary to "leap across the chasm that separates absolute idealism from dialectical materialism" (*Qu'est-ce que le Surréalisme?,* 1934). Breton had come to realize that automatic writing and drawing were inadequate forms of expression. Having read Trotsky's book about Lenin (Paris and Berlin, 1924), he began to understand the full extent of the historic importance of the Russian Revolution.

In its December 1925 issue, *Clarté* announced that it would discontinue publication and be replaced by a new magazine, *La Guerre civile.* It would be published jointly by the authors of *Clarté* and *La Révolution surréaliste* and would be the organ of the French left-wing intelligentsia. But, faced with the decision to give up his own magazine, Breton withdrew his offer of collaboration. *La Guerre civile* was never published because, while Breton wanted revolution, he also wanted to continue Surrealist experimentation

LA RÉVOLUTION SURRÉALISTE

Directeurs :
Pierre NAVILLE et Benjamin PÉRET
15, Rue de Grenelle
PARIS (7e)

Le surréalisme ne se présente pas comme l'exposition d'une doctrine. Certaines idées qui lui servent actuellement de point d'appui ne permettent en rien de préjuger de son développement ultérieur. Ce premier numéro de la Révolution Surréaliste *n'offre donc aucune révélation définitive. Les résultats obtenus par l'écriture automatique, le récit de rêve, par exemple, y sont représentés, mais aucun résultat d'enquêtes, d'expériences ou de travaux n'y est encore consigné : il faut tout attendre de l'avenir.*

23. Title page for *La Révolution surréaliste,* December 1, 1924

No 8 — Deuxième année — 1er Décembre 1926

LA RÉVOLUTION SURRÉALISTE

CE QUI MANQUE A TOUS CES MESSIEURS C'EST LA DIALECTIQUE (*ENGELS*)

SOMMAIRE

Revue de la Presse : P. Eluard et B. Péret
TEXTES SURRÉALISTES :
Pierre Unik, Cl.-A. Puget.
Moi l'abeille j'étais chevelure : Louis Aragon.
D. A. F. de Sade, écrivain fantastique et révolutionnaire : P. Eluard.
POÈMES
Max Morise, André Breton, Benjamin Péret, Michel Leiris.
Dzerjinski, président de la Tchéka : Pierre de Massot.
Lettre à la voyante : Antonin Artaud.
Opération : règle d'étroit : Pierre Brasseur.
Les dessous d'une vie ou la pyramide humaine : Paul Eluard.
Confession d'un enfant du siècle : Robert Desnos.
Uccello le poil : Antonin Artaud.
CHRONIQUES :
La saison des bains de ciel : G. Ribemont-Dessaignes.
Correspondance : Marcel Noll, E. Gengenbach.
Légitime défense : André Breton.
ILLUSTRATIONS :
Max Ernst, Georges Malkine, André Masson, Joan Miró, Man Ray, Yves Tanguy, Paolo Uccello.

ADMINISTRATION : 16, Rue Jacques-Callot, PARIS (VIe)

ABONNEMENT, les 12 Numéros : France : 55 francs Étranger : 100 francs

Dépositaire général : Librairie GALLIMARD 15, Boulevard Raspail, 15 PARIS (VIIe)

LE NUMÉRO : France : 5 francs Étranger : 7 francs

24. Title page for *La Révolution surréaliste,* December 1, 1926

25. Photograph of Breton, Eluard, Tzara, Péret (left to right). 1922

26. "The World at the Time of the Surrealists," from *Variétés,* 1929

in his own way. Instead of a joint venture, there would be reciprocal contributions. Until 1927, Aragon, Eluard, Desnos, and Péret contributed poems and essays to *Clarté,* which continued publication. Conversely, the authors of *Clarté* were represented by articles on social and political questions in the magazine of the Surrealists.

But the controversy did not end there. In 1926, Pierre Naville once again raised the question of what Surrealism's goal ought to be ("La Révolution et les intellectuels"). In his opinion, their spectacular demonstrations did nothing whatever for the proletariat. He contended that Surrealism was merely a matter of the intellect and that, furthermore, there was an irreconcilable contradiction between the Surrealists' metaphysical and dialectical attitudes. He questioned the possibility of "liberating the mind before the bourgeois order of material conditions of life had been removed . . . or does the liberation of the mind conversely presuppose the elimination of bourgeois control of the material conditions of life?"

Depending on how one answers this question of cause and effect, the conclusion to be drawn, according to Naville, would be one of two things: either cling to Anarchism which does not lead to revolution or, with complete dedication, take "the revolutionary road, the only revolutionary road, the Marxist road"; this would mean the end of individual experiments and the adoption of a collective struggle. Individualists cannot be revolutionaries. They can, at best, produce individual prophecies. Naville pleaded in favor of the Marxist way.

Breton admitted that Naville had created a great deal of unrest and uncertainty within the group. That same year, 1926, Breton published an article, "Légitime défense," which was not so much an answer to Naville's theories as an attack on the Communists, whom he didn't regard as true revolutionaries. As for the Surrealist position, Breton said: "There is not one among us who would not want to see the transfer of power from the hands of the bourgeoisie to those of the proletariat. But until that time comes, we still feel that experiences and experiments from the inner life of the individual should be continued. . . . We felt it would be senseless for us to become directly political, but we thought we could make ourselves useful in a general way instead by . . . constantly reminding the public of the basic principles of revolution."

The political élan of the preceding year had evaporated. By now, the Surrealists had confined themselves to desiring the revolution; they no longer wanted to work for it. While waiting for it to come about, they would continue their experiments of joining the conscious and the unconscious. Naville's suggestion had been rejected. As a result, he parted company with the Surrealists. At the same time, Aragon, Breton, Eluard, and Péret joined the Communist Party, ostensibly as a result of Naville's influence. Their move was probably caused by tactical considerations, after they had banned Artaud and Soupault from the Surrealist circle for having placed an autonomous value on literature.

While this controversy continued to rage, the Surrealists arranged a number of publications and exhibitions. The first Surrealist exhibition at the Galerie Pierre in Paris, in 1925, contained works by Arp, De Chirico, Max Ernst, Masson, Miró, Picasso, Man Ray, Pierre Roy, and Paul Klee, who had been adopted by the Surrealists, though he had shown absolutely no interest in their activities. A Man Ray exhibition opened

27. Robert Desnos. *Death of André Breton.* 1922

28. Max Morise. *Discovery of the Endless Screw.* 1925

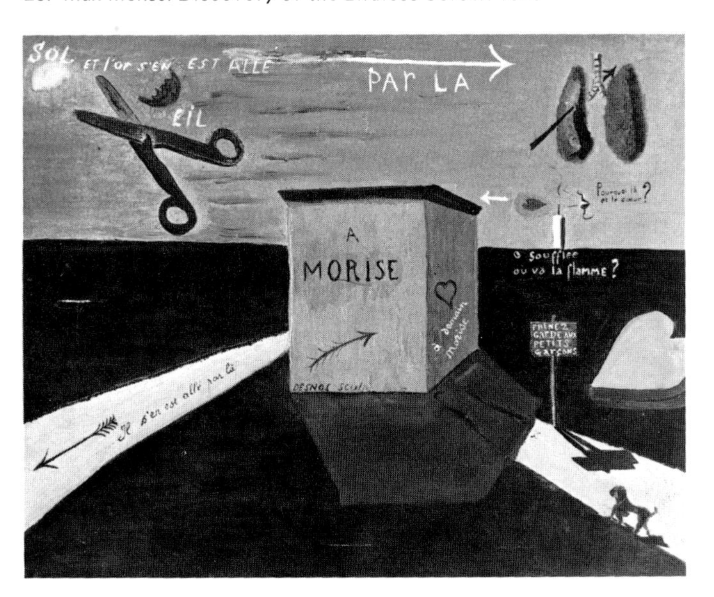

29. Robert Desnos. *Death of Max Morise.* 1923

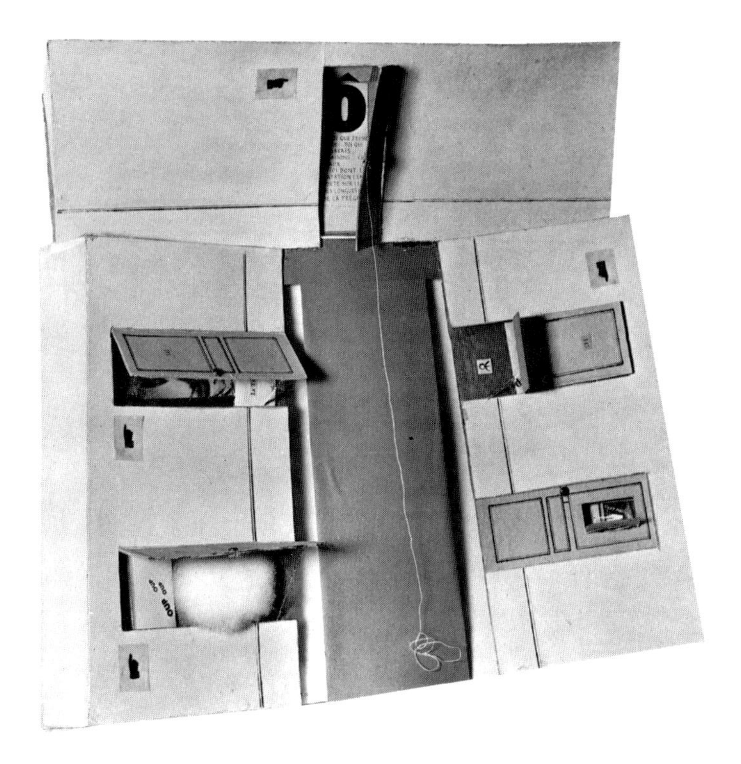

30. André Breton. *Dream Object.* 1935. Cardboard collage construction

the Galerie Surréaliste in Paris in 1926. That same year, Ernst's *frottages* appeared. Man Ray created the decor for the first act of *Romeo and Juliet* for Diaghilev's Ballets Russes; Ernst did the second act. This put them into disfavor with Aragon and Breton, who deplored their working with a *grand-bourgeois* White Russian. In 1927, Ernst (Galerie Van Leer) and Tanguy (Galerie Surréaliste)—who had become a member of the group—had exhibitions in Paris. Magritte, who lived near Paris from 1927 to 1930 and was close to Breton's circle during that time, showed his works in Brussels (Galerie Le Centaur). The first Surrealist films were appearing—by Dulac and Artaud, Man Ray, and Buñuel. In 1928, the Galerie Surréaliste held a De Chirico retrospective, while the Galerie Georges Bernheim in Paris showed Miró and, later, Ernst. At the Galerie Au Sacre du Printemps there was a Surrealist exhibition with works by Arp, De Chirico, Ernst, Malkine, Masson, Miró, Picabia, Roy, and Tanguy.

In 1929 some changes took place within the group that were important for its future. Desnos, Miró, Masson, and Prévert withdrew from it; Dali, Buñuel, René Char, Giacometti, and Tzara joined it. It was a year of turning points: *La Révolution surréaliste* appeared for the last time and its final issue contained Breton's second Surrealist manifesto. Apart from this, there were fewer activities. Max Ernst published his first picture novel, *La Femme 100 têtes*. Dali had his first one-man show at the Galerie Goemans in Paris.

The Second Manifesto, 1929

Up to the end of the 1920s, Surrealism had been a two-pronged movement. On the one hand, there had been theoretical, political, and increasingly more personal arguments, as well as proclamations and manifestos. On the other hand, there were the literary and pictorial products (no longer automatic) and films. All this had become established—at least in the minds of the Parisian art public—as the products of a serious artistic avant-garde. What strikes one at first glance about these artistic products is how widely they differ from each other in style and subject matter. We need only compare Aragon's descriptive "Paysan de Paris" with Breton's semidocumentary *Nadja*, or Magritte's semantic paintings with Miró's automatic pictures, to appreciate this divergence. Thus we see Surrealist theory occasionally unified, but Surrealist practice totally divergent within itself and furthermore quite often in complete disagreement with established Surrealist theory.

For this reason the theory of the Surrealists, as expressed primarily in the two manifestos, is somewhat less than helpful in the interpretation of texts, pictures and films. We cannot learn much from Surrealist theory beyond the general description of the method by which incongruous elements are combined, and even this information has to be culled from the first manifesto by means of interpretation. Perhaps Aragon realized that Surrealism had not explained itself sufficiently when,

31. Alberto Giacometti. *The Table.* 1933. Plaster

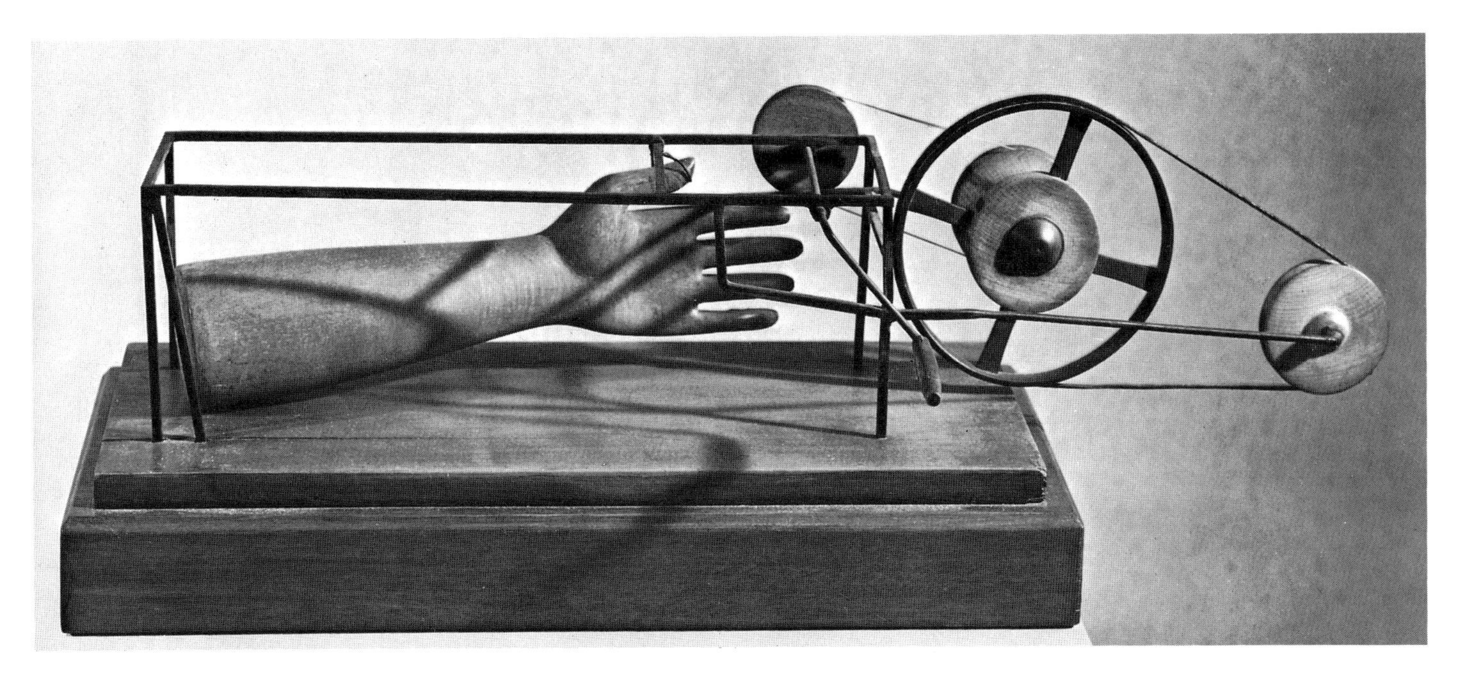

32. Alberto Giacometti. *Caught Hand.* 1932. Wood and metal

in 1928, he ironically suggested the following definition: "Surrealism is defined through those for whom it stands and through those who attack it" ("Traité du style").

The second manifesto offers no basic definitions or statements of purpose. It confines itself—due to the disparate structure of the movement and its practices—to correcting certain concepts and to emphasizing others within a body of established subjects. At the very beginning, this new manifesto takes a much more reticent and realistic view of what the Surrealist movement is all about than had hitherto been the case: "Regardless of the varied activities of all those who claim allegiance to Surrealism, it must be admitted that the movement's main ambition is to produce a general and serious *crisis of consciousness,* both in the intellectual and in the moral realm. Whether this goal is reached or not will determine the success or failure of the movement." The only dogma was "unconditional revolt, total disobedience, systematic sabotage."

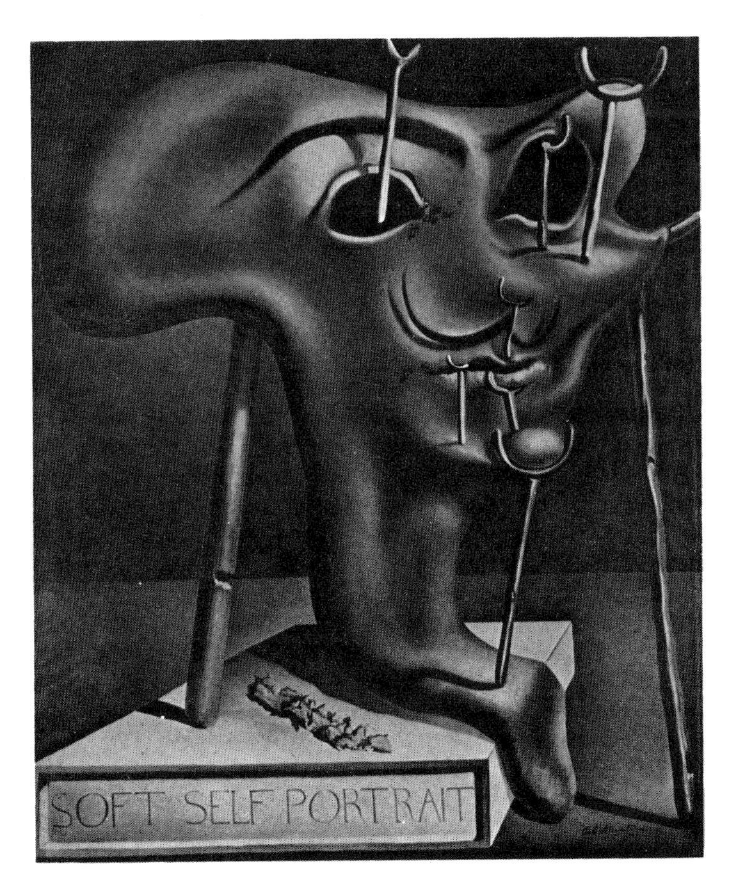

33. Salvador Dali. *Soft Self-Portrait with Fried Bacon.* 1941. Oil on canvas

As for the automatic texts, Breton now took the position that their producers had exerted too little control over them, and that this was why they were far less enlightening than had been hoped. Reading between the lines, one finds the demand for conscious manipulation of an unconscious process; in this respect Breton had long since been overtaken by actual practice, in both literature and art.

Breton now declared himself in favor of the social revolution which he saw as being compatible with Surrealism. However, he shared a rather widespread belief that only failures would dedicate themselves to political agitation. Still, he did arrive at a well differentiated view of the relationship that exists between art and literature on the one hand and the working class on the other. Referring to Trotsky's essay "Literature and Revolution" (1923), Breton wrote: "I do not believe that there is, at present, a possibility for the existence of any literature or art that expresses the aims of the working class . . . because in any period preceding revolution, the writers or artists are necessarily of bourgeois extraction and therefore incapable of being spokesmen for working-class aims . . . I consider all attempts at defending or illustrating a so-called proletarian art or literature quite wrong at a time when no one can point to a proletarian culture, for the simple reason that no such culture exists, not even under a proletarian regime." Apparently, Trotsky's ideas had a strong effect on Breton, whose many statements frequently have the effect of obscuring things rather than elucidating them.

The purification of Surrealism, which Breton hoped to accomplish with his second manifesto, was no longer possible, for it had long since turned into a movement of the arts, of literature and film, far removed from any unification of art and life, and even further removed from any real revolutionary goals. The second manifesto reinforced Breton's standing as the theoretician of the group, but it did not strengthen his position as its leader. Still, it was he who had held the movement together, a movement whose very contradictoriness, in questions of art as well as of socio-politics, had become its trademark.

Unconscious Notation—The Principle of Metamorphosis

Breton's definition of Surrealism in his first manifesto shows that, at least in the beginning, he had considered Surrealism and automatism identical. His orientation was toward literature: "At that time I was still intensely preoccupied with Freud and was familiar with his method of investigation, which I had been able to apply to some of my patients in the war. I got from myself what they had been asked for: a free-flowing, fast monologue that was not subject to critical reason and therefore free from restraint. It was to be as close to *spoken thought* as possible. . . . With this understanding we—Philippe Soupault and I—began to cover quantities of paper with drawing and writing, regardless of what the literary result might be" (Manifesto, 1924).

The result: "The same errors of construction, the same weaknesses but, for both of us, an illusion of extraordinary élan, strong emotion, a remarkably large selection of pictures that were better than any we had been able to produce after long preparation, something peculiarly painterly, and now and then an extremely funny idea" (Manifesto, 1924).

AUTOMATIC WRITING

Automatic writing—this "Surrealist game," this "form of pure expression" (Breton)—became the rage among writers; then the painters took it up. It was a method with even less aim and direction than collage. It was regarded as a method of writing or drawing that liberated the creative forces, not as a means for producing certain planned texts or pictures. These "liberating procedures serve the journey of discovery into the unconscious" (Ernst). The idea was to lay bare the "mechanism of poetic inspiration" and to unmask "moral or aesthetic considerations as hostile to inspiration" (Ernst). The procedure was important, not the product. The production of texts or pictures was no longer separate from everyday life. Everyone, not only the artist, could use automatic writing in order to liberate his personal potential: "Poetry must be made by all" (Lautréamont).

Since Breton initially put so much emphasis on automatic writing, it must be recognized as one of the keys to understanding Surrealism. Essential to it are: the supremacy of method over product; the neglect, even the rejection of any aesthetic criteria; and the bringing of art into the sphere of everyday life, in other words, artlessness.

From 1922 on, writers practiced automatic writing and painters produced automatic drawings. Among the latter were Masson, Miró, Tanguy, and also, on occasion, Ernst (figs. 34–37). Their drawings, free-flowing like handwriting, and containing many objective forms, make one wonder just how unconscious their production really was. It seems rather as if unconscious jottings and squiggles had been the starting points and inspiration for the more careful definition (metamorphosis) of certain figures and objects. In that case, automatic writing or drawing would not be the purely spontaneous act it was purported to be, but rather a method to produce such a spontaneous act and then to categorize it. In this way, the method would be rationally applied. This element of conscious control is what Breton admitted in his first manifesto and demanded in his second manifesto. Automatic writing and automatic drawing shall therefore be classified as semiautomatic procedures that can liberate the imagination and get inspiration started. In the same way, Ernst's *frottage* and *grattage*, and the collage method developed by Oscar Dominguez, are to be understood as variations on the method of semiautomatic drawing.

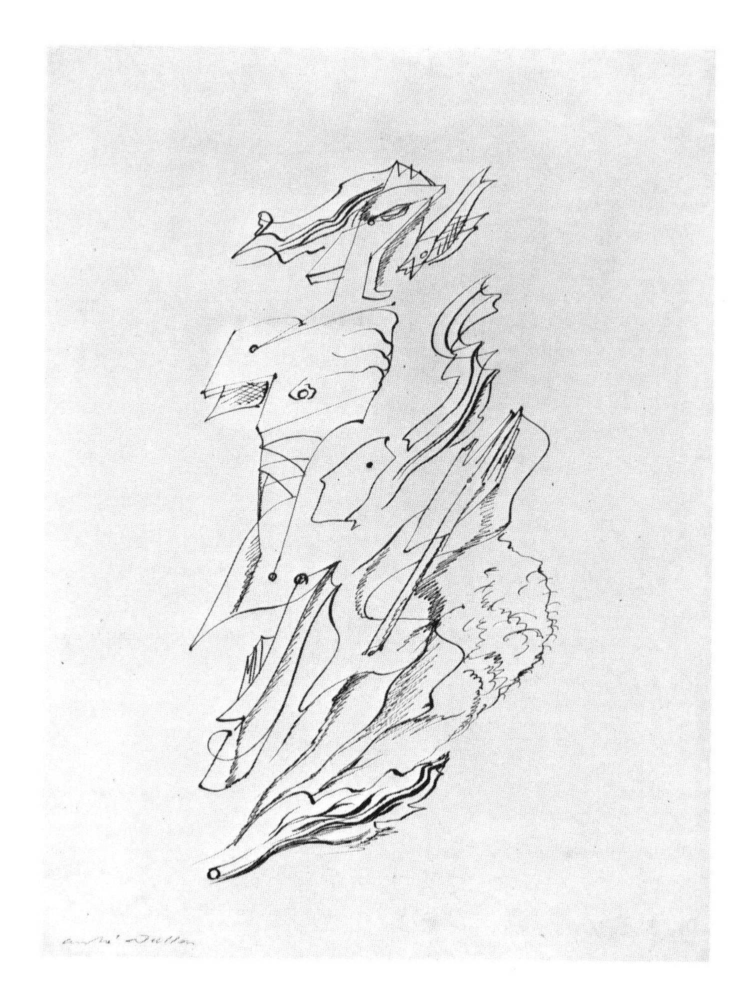

34. André Masson. *A Knight*. 1925

35. Joan Miró. *The Writer.* 1924. Pencil and watercolor

36. Joan Miró. *Automaton.* 1924. Pen and ink

Peter Bürger recently commented on the interpretation of semiautomatic texts and drawings:

> If the automatic texts really had the status of dream contents, as many critics insist, there would be only one way to interpret them, in the Freudian sense. The existing text would correspond to the manifest dream content and we would have to use it to discover the unconscious thought behind it, which would correspond to the latent dream content. But we could do that only if we knew the writer's experiences immediately preceding notation, by means of free association. This means that, if we regard automatic writing as strictly analogous to dreaming, we wouldn't be able to interpret it at all. But Breton himself does not see automatic writing as analogous to dreaming but rather to Freud's technique of free association. We must therefore approach the idea that automatic writing expresses the Unconscious, directly or distorted as a dream does, with extreme caution (bibl. 48).

Bürger has further pointed out that "whatever preoccupied the Surrealists in their conscious minds also dominated their automatic texts."

What Breton envisioned and Max Ernst postulated of semimechanical and later of semiautomatic drawing and writing was a quasi-scientific task, the exploration of the mechanics of inspiration. But these novel techniques were not really suited for such a purpose. Psychoanalysis could do the job much more efficiently and effectively. Still, automatic writing pointed in the right direction: it certainly helped many participating artists discover new forms; it gave rise to the development of several other semiautomatic techniques—from *frottage* to *fumage* (Paalen; fig. 59)—and it played a seminal part in the new evaluation of artistic creativity which the Surrealists were the first to apply.

The importance of the evocative character of these semiautomatic and semimechanical methods for the art of the twentieth century cannot be overemphasized. During their "automatic" phase, Max Ernst and many of his successors regarded most of their picture-producing activities as suggestions, not solutions—an outgrowth of their general antiart philosophy.

It is characteristic of Surrealism that its ideas are continuously in a state of transition (Breton himself, though for reasons of his own, said in his second manifesto in 1929 that Surrealism was still in its preparatory phase). It could never fully realize itself, because the original problem, the alienation of life from art, cannot be solved within the framework of art. Surrealism had to keep constantly in motion, in transition, open to change. It had to remain pluralistic and contradictory; in fact, pluralism and contradiction were its guiding principles. These evocative qualities became its trademark. Thus we must see Surrealism not as the realization of an idea, but as an idea that has not yet been executed. Its long-range influence can be observed in the fact that during the events of May 1968, in Paris, Surrealist slogans appeared on the walls of public buildings. It can also be observed in the Flux Panels by Ben Vautier, for example (*Ben Is Art,* 1964), which may have been inspired by Péret's "Art does not exist; Art, that's Us"; in Claes Oldenburg's fictive alterations of cities which most likely hark back to Breton's suggestions for ways of rearranging Paris; or in Conceptual Art which can be traced back to the conceptual drawings of Méret Oppenheim (figs. 58, 61). And we can see an interesting comeback of semiautomatic, "artless" drawing in the works of Henri Michaux and Joseph Beuys. The principle of artlessness which Duchamp, Dada, and Surrealism brought to art probably exerts a greater influence on today's art than does any other idea: in Object Art, in Earth Art, in the realm of Happenings, the real is provocatively displayed as an aesthetic object.

Altogether, the seminal strength of Surrealism is not based on model achievements or specific forms, but on the principle of unresolved conflict—both on the level of realization (collage, montage, incongruous combination, metamorphosis) and on the theoretical level (contrast between art and life, between collective social action and individualism). This conflict is exposed and not brought into harmony; it is regarded as a driving force and must remain unresolved. The mainte-

37. Yves Tanguy. *Automatic Drawing.* 1926

nance of unresolved conflict gave a central impetus to Surrealism and to many subsequent trends in art which demanded that art not be satisfying but stimulating, not harmonious but full of doubt and irritation.

LE CADAVRE EXQUIS

Another "Surrealist game" in which disparate elements are joined as in collage into a self-contradictory whole is *le cadavre exquis* (exquisite corpse) (1924–25). This is how the *Dictionnaire abrégé du Surréalisme* of 1938 describes it: "A game with folded paper. Every participant makes a drawing without knowing what his predecessor has drawn, because the predecessor's contribution is concealed by the folded part of the paper. The example which has become a classic, and to which the game owes its name, was the first sentence produced by this method: *'Le cadavre exquis boira le vin nouveau'* [The exquisite corpse will drink the new wine]." Of course, the hybrid products of this game would be unthinkable without the Surrealists' antiart striving. What makes the game interesting is not any one artistic product but the collective playfulness and the incongruous combination of text and picture; the latter resulted in a shape made continuous by the fact that players extended their lines beyond the folded part of the paper. These shapes were partly abstract, partly organic. It is, of course, completely impossible to interpret these products. To the outsider they bear witness to the fun the artists must have had in making them, and to the way in which this game supported their efforts at breaking through the boundaries of artistic tradition and at appearing altogether and collectively antiart. The *cadavre exquis* had a kind of predecessor in the Fatagaga collages which Hans Arp and Max Ernst produced during their Cologne Dada period, except that in Fatagaga each knew what the other was doing.

The underlying principle of the *cadavre exquis* is metamorphosis, unconsciously achieved. A remark made by Max Ernst shows that this, too, was considered a liberating act: "The pleasure derived from successful metamorphosis has nothing to do with a miserable, aesthetic desire for distraction. It has to do with the vital need of the intellect to be liberated from the false, tedious paradise of permanent memories, to be able to explore a new, far greater realm of experience" (bibl. 25).

Whereas collage, montage, and their derivatives are based on the principle of incongruous combination, automatic drawing, *cadavre exquis, frottage,* decalcomania, and their derivatives are based on the principle of metamorphosis. Incongruous combination and metamorphosis are the two major principles of Surrealism; both are rational procedures that can yield irrational results.

The Verism of the Improbable—The Principle of Conscious Incongruous Combination

The idea of automatism and the idea of dream-painting—which Breton proclaimed as late as 1938, in his *Dictionnaire abrégé du Surréalisme,* when he called for the "realistic reproduction of dream images"—typify two distinctly different branches of Surrealism. About 1925, one branch consisted of those artists who worked with semiautomatic methods, influenced by literary procedures. The early Tanguy, Masson, and Miró belong in this group. On the other side we find, toward the end of the twenties, the Verists of the Improbable: Tanguy, Magritte, and Dali, whose influences had been De Chirico and the early Max Ernst.

The artists of both branches—regardless of the tremendous differences between them—together represent what is called Surrealist painting. If we took Surrealist theory at its face value, however, the designation "Surrealist painting" would be self-contradictory. The first Surrealist manifesto states that Surrealism goes "beyond all aesthetic . . . considerations," that it aims to be a complete social program rather than merely an artistic one. Although automatic drawing and *cadavre exquis* may well have remained completely outside of all artistic tradition, at least for a while, verism was a different matter. Aesthetic considerations had to be respected first and foremost in veristic painting. These pictures are nothing if not art, a continuation of the history of easel painting, even though they may introduce completely new values.

This contradiction between antiart theory and art-producing practice did not go undetected by the Surrealists themselves. In the third issue of *La Révolution surréaliste,* in 1925, Pierre Naville wrote: "All matters of taste give me nothing but a disgusting aftertaste. You Masters! You Meistersingers! Go ahead and slop paint all over your canvases! Sooner or later everyone will know that there is no such thing as *Surrealist painting!* Neither the scribbling of a pencil haphazardly moved by a hand which the unconscious guides, nor pictures reproducing creatures and objects of dreams, nor any other fantastic, arbitrary productions can be summed up by such a designation."

The artists, of course, took a dim view of Naville's position. They were just outgrowing the stage of pure experimentation; they had developed a kind of art that was being appreciated, that was, in a manner of speaking, becoming respectable. While it was not altogether synonymous with the ideas of Surrealism, it was nevertheless based on them. While the picture-making methods of some of these artists might be somewhat distant from Surrealist theory, they did consider themselves Surrealists, especially as they owed a great deal of inspiration to its ideas.

But the contradiction remained. Three years after Naville's outburst, Breton wrote about Surrealism and painting (*Le Surréalisme et la peinture,* 1928) without calling the book "Surrealist painting." In his manifestos he never mentioned the graphic arts, except for some references connected with automatism. Breton's ideas about painting were rather vague. In *Les Pas perdus* (1924), he had expressed appreciation of Moreau, Gauguin, Seurat, Redon, Picasso, De Chirico, and Max Ernst. In his 1924 manifesto, he mentions—without discussing any aesthetic points—Matisse, Derain, Klee, Braque, Man Ray, and, again, De Chirico and Ernst, as well as Masson. Very likely this vagueness on Breton's part contributed to the fact that the artists did not feel as closely attached to the group as the writers did.

It is interesting to note that Max Ernst, who occupies a special position between the two separate branches of Surrealism, remarked in an interview many years later: "I must confess that I kept at a certain distance from the experiments and doctrines of the Surrealists. . . . I doubted that one could 'change' the world by artistic means or verbal utopias" (bibl. 95). Apparently, none of the artists completely accepted Surrealism as a philosophy of life. They arrived at their so-called "Irritations" (Ernst) in the wake of Surrealist theory. These pictorial "Irritations," along with writings and films, represent the Surrealism of the twenties and thirties to us today.

"A certain distance," as Ernst called it, can be seen in the veristic pictures, too. Neither Tanguy, Magritte, or Dali actually painted dreams. Tanguy, in his gently sloping, often horizonless landscapes of precise shading, carefully and artfully combined biomorphic objects and their mysterious shadows. We perceive, behind Tanguy's work, the stage sets,

38–39. Examples of *cadavre exquis*

monuments, and shadows of De Chirico, with their conscious, deliberate mystification of the viewer. These pictures were not used for purposes of self-discovery. They were objects produced for aesthetic, though "mysterious," enjoyment. The emptiness, lifelessness, and uncertainty of these pictures was consciously produced illusionism.

For Magritte, the conscious act of recognition was the very basis of painting. It is his method that is illusionistic. The objects in his pictures appear real. By the principle of incongruous combination, he brings several different levels of thought together, in connection with the objects depicted: the word as symbol, the word as idea, the picture as symbol, the picture as idea, the word as picture, the picture as word. "This is not a pipe," says the legend on a picture that shows a pipe and is titled *The Wind and the Song.* The underlying thought about the function and possibility of language and picture is very precise. There are no dreams in these pictures. The enigmatic effect is deliberate, planned.

Salvador Dali, in his early pictures—done in the twenties, before he began to indulge in self-mystification—painted what he knew of Freud and Freudian methods. Therefore, it would be completely wrong to interpret these pictures by applying the psychoanalytical method. After all, they deliberately use the findings of psychoanalysis and apply them to the artist's own childhood. Sigmund Freud himself was aware of this. When Dali visited him in 1928 and showed him photographs of his paintings, Freud said: "In your pictures I seek the conscious, not the unconscious. In the old masters—Leonardo or Ingres—what interests me and seems mysterious and disquieting is the search for unconscious, enigmatic ideas, concealed in the picture. In your case, the mystery is on the surface. The picture is merely a mechanism for uncovering the mystery" (Dali, *The Secret Life of Salvador Dali,* New York, 1942). It would be hard to give a better description of the difference between the theory and practice of Surrealism, between Dali's deliberate mystification and the reality of his pictorial world.

The essence of "automatic" drawing and of illusionistic "dream" pictures does not lie in any unconscious production method, nor in dream-reporting. It lies in the conscious exploitation of semiautomatic processes and in the conscious creation of pictures that seem like mysterious dreams, based on familiarity with psychoanalysis. These Surrealist pictures are not called into being instead of, but with the help of, psychoanalysis.

Max Ernst, the Individualist—The Puzzle Principle

Max Ernst's role has frequently been mentioned in this book. It was he who perfected the collage technique, which anticipated the principle of incongruous combination—a principle that forms a link between Dada and Surrealism. Ernst also worked out a whole series of semiautomatic processes that were based on the principle of metamorphosis. These techniques went beyond dogmatic Surrealist theory, though they were clearly influenced and inspired by it.

In 1921, Eluard met Ernst in Cologne and almost instantly bought the proto-Surrealist *The Elephant Celebes* which Ernst had painted that year (colorplate 4). In 1922 they jointly published "Répétitions" and "Les Malheurs des Immortels" in Paris. Two years before, Breton had suggested that Ernst exhibit his work in Paris, and Ernst had done so, at the Galerie Au Sans Pareil. The exhibition was called *Beyond Painting.* Its opening turned into a Dada demonstration in which Aragon, Breton, and Tzara took part. Yet, in 1924, when Breton—in his first manifesto—mentioned the names of those who had been sworn to his program, he did not include Max Ernst (who had moved to Paris in 1922). Ernst was out of the country when the magazine *La Révolution surréaliste* and the Bureau de Recherches Surréalistes were founded, and as a rule his name is absent from group proclamations and pamphlets—the one exception being a protest against French military intervention in Morocco. Ernst, who in 1969 emphasized that "certain distance"

40. Yves Tanguy. *Untitled, II.* 1935

LES MOTS ET LES IMAGES

Un objet ne tient pas tellement à son nom qu'on ne puisse lui en trouver un autre qui lui convienne mieux :

le canon

Il y a des objets qui se passent de nom :

Un mot ne sert parfois qu'à se désigner soi-même :

ciel

Un objet rencontre son image, un objet rencontre son nom. Il arrive que l'image et le nom de cet objet se rencontrent :

forêt

Parfois le nom d'un objet tient lieu d'une image :

canon

Un mot peut prendre la place d'un objet dans la réalité :

le soleil

Une image peut prendre la place d'un mot dans une proposition :

Le est caché par les nuages

Un objet fait supposer qu'il y en a d'autres derrière lui :

Tout tend à faire penser qu'il y a peu de relation entre un objet et ce qui le représente :

l'objet réel l'objet représenté

Les mots qui servent à désigner deux objets différents ne montrent pas ce qui peut séparer ces objets l'un de l'autre :

personnage perdant la mémoire corps de femme

Dans un tableau, les mots sont de la même substance que les images :

Dans un tableau, les mots sont de la même substance que les images :

On voit autrement les images et les mots dans un tableau :

montagne

Une forme quelconque peut remplacer l'image d'un objet :

le soleil le soleil le soleil

Un objet ne fait jamais le même office que son nom ou que son image :

cheval

Or, les contours visibles des objets, dans la réalité, se touchent comme s'ils formaient une mosaïque :

Les figures vagues ont une signification aussi nécessaire aussi parfaite que les précises :

Parfois, les noms écrits dans un tableau désignent des choses précises, et les images des choses vagues :

canon

Ou bien le contraire :

brouillard

René MAGRITTE.

above: 41. René Magritte. "Words and Pictures," from *La Révolution surréaliste*, December 15, 1929

right: 42. René Magritte. *Key of Dreams*. 1930. Oil on canvas

below: 43. Salvador Dali. *How the Surrealist Saw Broadway*. 1935

which he kept from the Surrealist movement, is nevertheless one of its most important figures. His contribution to the provocative and stimulating variety of Surrealism is enormous.

To look for a uniform style in Ernst's work would be as fruitless as looking for a uniform style of Surrealism. What matters is not style, or any question of form, but method of creation. The product is the result of technical manipulation. Consciously conceived, but with enough room for accident, it is ambiguous in meaning and produces associative possibilities in the viewer. The work is set in motion by the technical process. The viewer, in turn, is set in motion by the result, which still shows traces of the process that began it all. This relationship between product and viewer we can call *inspirative*.

Ernst is no more a painter of dreams and unconscious profundities than is any other Surrealist. Familiar with the mechanisms of dreams and humor, as analyzed by Freud, he playfully alludes to history and art history, presents psychological fusions, apparent hallucinations, concrete materials, and certain new procedural methods; he combines disparate levels of civilization and reality, or puts new meaning into alienated, purposeless structures and so creates—his antiart attitude notwithstanding—works of art.

Ernst studied at a university, not an academy of art. Like Magritte, he is an intellectual artist. In studying the history of art, he showed a decided preference for Mannerism and the Romantics; he reacted to the events of his own time with

44. Salvador Dali. *City of Drawers.* 1936 (the same motif occurs in *Burning Giraffe* of 1935 and in his sculpture, *Venus de Milo of the Drawers,* of 1936)

45. Marie Toyen. Drawing from the series *Le Tir.* 1939–40

unconcealed hatred for the authoritarianism that had oppressed his childhood and youth, and showed equal hatred for war, church, and dictatorship.

Instead of painting pictures with a brush, Ernst used complicated but comprehensible methods of production which changed the character of picture-making: inspiration was merely the act of making things visible. "As a last superstition, a sad remnant of the myth of creation, there remains in Western culture the fairy tale of the artist's creativity. One of the revolutionary acts of Surrealism was a sober and extremely sharp attack on that myth, which may have eradicated it once and for all" (Ernst, in bibl. 25). Ernst's critical mind denied the existence of art in the traditional sense, yet he produced art in constantly new ways, none of which he ever drove to perfection. This antinomy, which he never abandoned, was one of the main operative forces in his work. When Picasso said of himself that he did not seek but found, Ernst replied that *he* did not find—he sought. There are no solutions for Ernst, only contradictions and tensions, and this is precisely what gives his work its inspiring power.

The systematic transmogrification of materials, shapes,

and trivial pictures, and the reinterpretation of art and artistry as practiced by Max Ernst demand the same kind of active, intellectual participation from the viewer required by a picture puzzle—the kind of trick picture that "contains a figure that is not instantly recognizable."

In this respect, Ernst's work comes much closer to automatic drawing than to the perfect execution and formal uniformity of Dali's pictures. Full of scruples, skepticism, and humor, Ernst's work is open, stimulating, entertaining. He consciously exploits the ambiguity of objects and structures for purposes of puzzlement, in his *frottages, grattages,* wood-block collages, decalcomania, and various thematic inventions between 1925 and 1940. And again—as in collage, semiautomatic drawings, and incongruous combination—the methods he employs are rational but the results can be unpredictable, surprising, and often dependent on the viewer's own contribution.

The puzzle picture is the result of pictorial procedures by which certain objects or structures become divorced from their original functions. This is the montage principle, in which unrelated elements are combined. But, at the same time, it also fits in with the metamorphosis principle, because familiar objects are turned into something new and unknown (see Hans Holländer). Like Dali, Magritte, Roy, or Tanguy, Ernst gets an ambiguous-appearing response from reality by combining or transforming real-looking elements into new, improbable structures that have the character of probability because they are executed with illusionist finesse. When stood on its head in this way, reality itself becomes doubtful. This is what Breton means when, in his preface to Ernst's 1929 picture novel *La Femme 100 têtes,* he says: "The surreal is a function of our will to alienate everything." Alienation contains the potential of knowing the thing that has been alienated.

This is something which all Surrealist pictures, objects, and films have in common. They turn against the familiar, make it questionable, and weaken it by setting up enigmatic situations. Surrealist art does not affirm anything—it goes

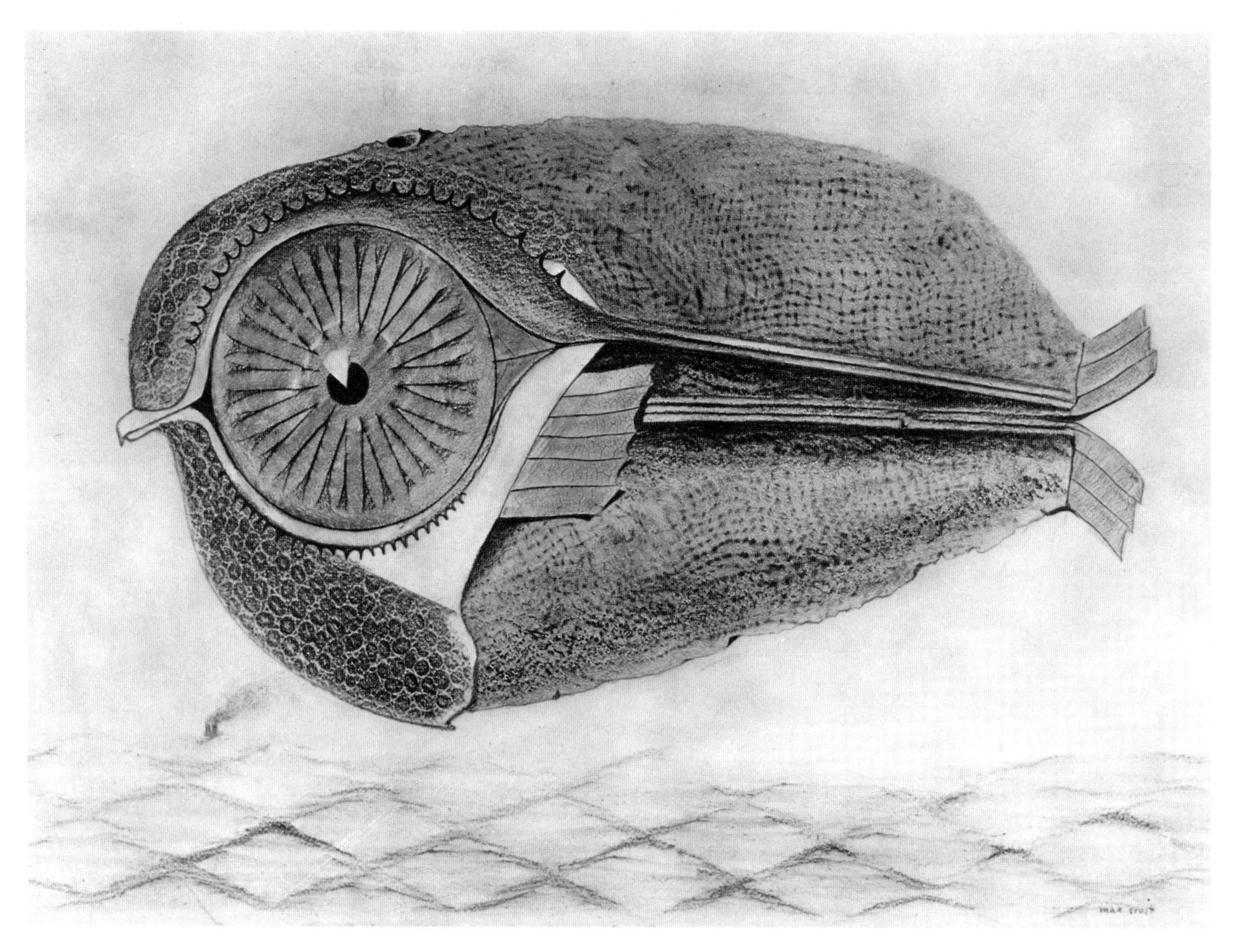

46. Max Ernst. *The Fugitive* (from *Histoire naturelle*). 1926. *Frottage*

against the grain. It does not contribute to a state of order; it questions such a state with creative distrust. Dali has said that his "whole ambition in the pictorial domain is to materialize the images of concrete irrationality with the most imperialistic fury of precision." These pictures, together with other Surrealist activities, were meant to "contribute to the total discrediting of the world of reality" (bibl. 43).

In his second manifesto, Breton wrote: "What Surrealism

47. Max Ernst. *Loplop Introduces a Young Girl.* 1931. Assemblage

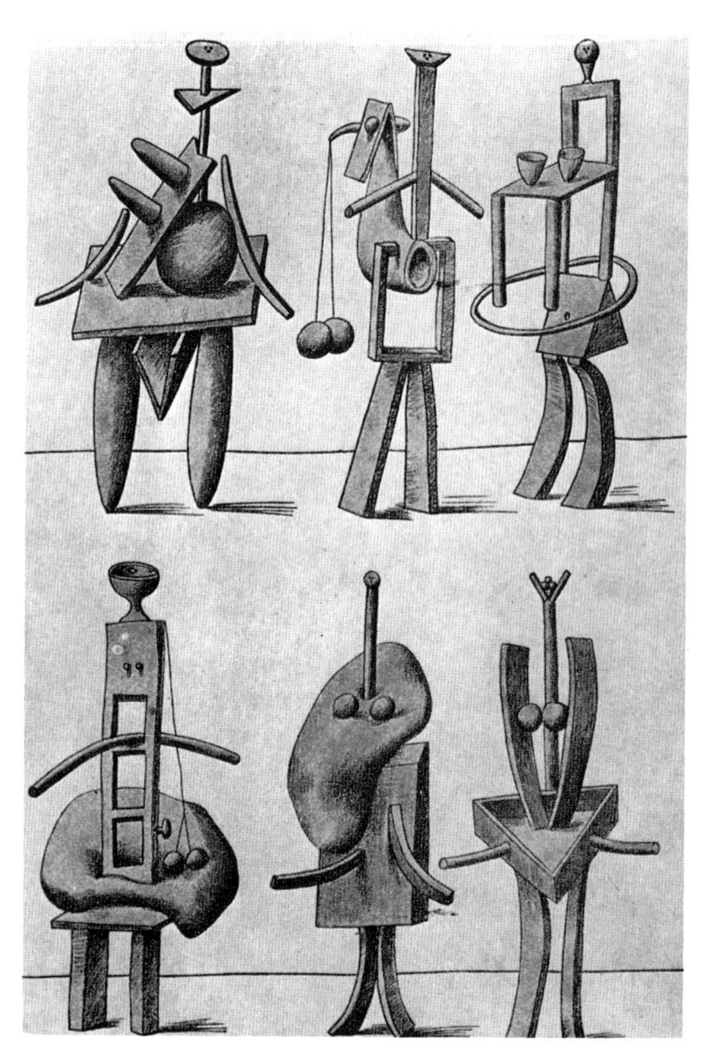

48. Pablo Picasso. *An Anatomy.* 1933. Pencil drawings from *Minotaure*

is aiming at, morally and intellectually . . . [is to] effect a *crisis of consciousness* of the most emphatic and general kind." And Max Ernst has written: "By turning the relationships of 'realities' to each other upside down it [the Surrealist movement] merely helped speed up the general crisis of conscience and consciousness of our time" (bibl. 25). These are extravagant claims. The effect of the movement was felt mainly in the world of art. Nevertheless, the element of opposition and provocation remains one of the chief characteristics of Surrealism and of those movements that succeeded it—in spirit, if not in form.

Films—The Principle of Shock-Montage

Since this is, essentially, a book about Surrealist painting, it would lead too far afield to discuss the literature of the period in detail. But a word must be said here about Surrealist films, as many Surrealist painters took part in their making. The listing for *film* in the *Dictionnaire abrégé du Surréalisme* of 1938 includes *Emak Bakia* (1927) by Man Ray; *L'Etoile de Mer* (1928) by Man Ray and Desnos; *Anemic Cinema* (1926) by Duchamp, Man Ray, and Marc Allégret; *La Perle* (1929) by Georges Hugnet; *Un Chien Andalou* (1928) and *L'Age d'or* (1930) by Luis Buñuel and Salvador Dali. One might add *La Coquille et le clergyman* (1927) by Germaine Dulac and Antonin Artaud, and *Mystères du château de dé* (1929) by Man Ray. Aragon, Breton, and Péret had planned films, but these were never produced. Among Dada precursors, one might mention *Le Retour à la raison* (1923) by Man Ray and *Entr'acte* (1924) by Francis Picabia and René Clair.

All these films were independently produced, noncommercial films. Together with Fernand Léger's *Ballet mécanique* (1924) they represent French avant-garde film art of the 1920s. It was inspired by artists and writers; it was deliberately experimental and opposed to the prevailing taste in film-making; it eschewed the kind of technical perfection that had become a common feature of popular films. Likewise, it did without elaborate stories and without narrative continuity.

The prototype of all Surrealist films was probably Picabia's *Entr'acte,* a work that had been commissioned for the ballet *Relâche,* which was performed by the Ballets Suèdois (Rolf de Maré) in 1924. The music for the ballet was written by Erik Satie; Jean Borlin did the choreography, Francis Picabia the scenery. Among the performers were Jean Borlin and Marcel Duchamp. *Entr'acte,* with a scenario by Picabia and a group of actors that included Borlin, Duchamp, Man Ray, and Picabia himself, is a two-part film. The first part consists of a seemingly accidental sequence of absurd, fragmentary scenes. The second part, which shows the pursuit of a hearse, employs a whole string of the latest camera techniques. The absurd action turns into a Dada joke.

Man Ray's *Le Retour à la raison* (1923) is a film made without a camera, by the Rayogram principle. In *Emak Bakia* (1927), Man Ray combined abstract light reflections with actual photography. Duchamp, in *Anemic Cinema,* combined his abstract rotoreliefs with puns and palindromes. A new note was struck by Dulac's *La Coquille et le clergyman* (1927); it is a collage narration full of sexual symbols, describing the bourgeois inhibited relationship between a priest and a woman, with continual interruptions by a monstrous general. Artaud, who wrote the scenario, later explained his intentions in a rather revealing way: "The scenario is not the story of a dream. I won't try to make excuses for its lack of continuity by pretending that it was meant to be a dream. The scenario tried to describe the dark truth of the soul . . . each image evolves out of the preceding one . . . these images create their own autonomous world. And out of the totality of images, out of a metamorphosis of elements, an anorganic language develops which enters our consciousness by osmosis and needs no translation into words" (bibl. 73).

L'Etoile de mer (1928) by Man Ray is based on a poem by Robert Desnos. Like most of its predecessors, it has no continuity of action. Pictures of starfish are combined with lines from the poem and with short action scenes. The alienating effect of this montage is deepened by the alternate use of

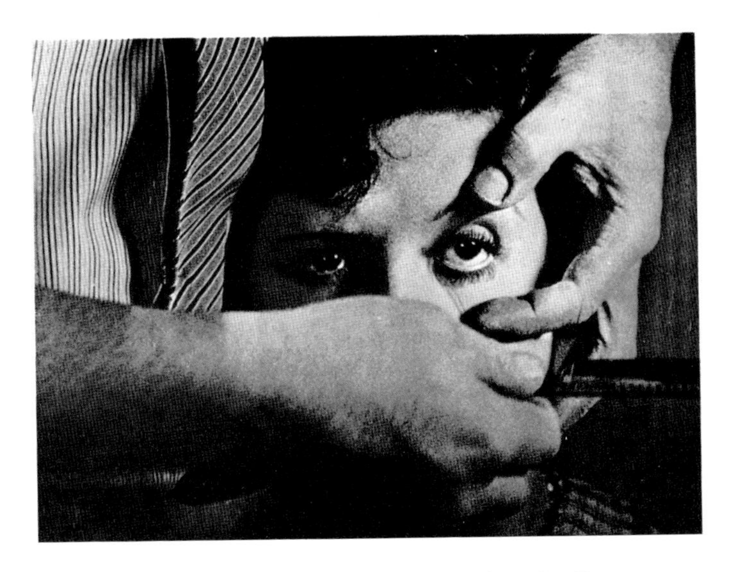

49. Luis Buñuel and Salvador Dali. Opening scene from the film *Un Chien Andalou.* 1928

50. Luis Buñuel and Salvador Dali. From the film *Un Chien Andalou* (ants are a frequently occurring motif with Dali). 1928

51. Luis Buñuel. From the film *L'Age d'or.* 1930

pictures in focus (mainly of the starfish) and out-of-focus photographs taken through a pane of glass. The abrupt shifts from one level to another and the fact that all three levels are given equal value make the total effect of the film enigmatic. On the action level (which shows an encounter between a man and a woman), nothing happens the way the audience expects it. The characters behave quite differently from what one has been led to assume in the opening scenes. In *Les Mystères du château de dé* (the title is an allusion to Mallarmé's poem "Un Coup de dés"), there is no continuous action either, though the beginning of the film leads us to expect it. Man Ray used the kind of camera work that was experimental at the time, such as superimposed images, slow-motion and reverse-motion sequences, to show some meaningless gymnastic exercises being performed by the masked guests at a palace of the Vicomte de Noailles. Similar camera work was used by Picabia, though in a less systematic way.

LUIS BUNUEL

Un Chien Andalou (1928) and *L'Age d'or* (1930) were the most accomplished of all Surrealist films. Both were by Buñuel, in collaboration with Dali. *Un Chien Andalou* was acted by Pierre Batcheff, Buñuel, and Dali, among others. It opens with a cruel scene, described as follows in the shooting script: "A balcony. Night. A man on the balcony is sharpening a razor. The man looks at the sky through a window and sees . . . a slim cloud approaching the full moon. Then the head of a young woman with wide-open eyes. Now the cloud moves across the moon. The razor blade cuts through the young woman's eye, severing it." The scene is called "Once upon a Time. . . ."

And the final scene ("In the Springtime"): "Everything has changed. We now see an endless desert. The man and the young woman in the center of the picture are buried up to their chests in sand; blinded, in rags, they are tormented by the sun and by swarms of insects."

Buñuel dispenses with logically developing action and with camera tricks. The sequences follow upon each other in a provocative way. They are deliberately absurd and senseless: "Dali and I used every gag that occurred to us, and we relentlessly threw out everything that might have meaning" (Buñuel). The music intensifies the shock value of the picture sequences; at the first performance of the silent film, there was music by Beethoven and Wagner, and a tango.

The interaction of image and motion and of image and sound in *Un Chien Andalou* is derived from Surrealist ideas which Buñuel himself admitted had meant a great deal to him. There is one important difference, though: the film does not show dreams, but utilizes the mechanism of dreams which Freud had discovered. "The action is the result of *conscious* psychic automation, and in this sense it does not try to narrate a dream, though it utilizes the same kind of mechanism that dreams utilize. The sources from which this film draws its inspiration are the sources of poetry that has freed itself from the ballast of tradition and reason" (Buñuel, 1961). Shock is considered a legitimate device for upsetting the viewer's equilibrium.

52. Luis Buñuel. Still with Gaston Modot from the film *L'Age d'or*. 1930

L'Age d'or, Buñuel's first talking film, was produced by the Vicomte de Noailles. The scenario is credited to Buñuel and Dali, but this is not quite accurate. Dali had meant to glorify the Catholic church; Buñuel turned the film into an anticlerical statement. It has been said that Dali's only contribution to the film is the sight gag showing a man who takes a walk with a loaf of bread on his head. The actors are Lya Lys, Gaston Modot, Max Ernst, and others.

The film is based on the collage principle. It borrows from documentary films (the opening scene, about scorpions), from news reportage (views of the Vatican, mass scenes with police), from Magritte (the mirror scene), from Freud (sex symbols), and from the Marquis de Sade (the palace scene at the end of the film, which uses De Sade's novel *The 120 Days of Sodom*). In a jumble of cruel and angry scenes, it attacks everything that is sacred to the bourgeois.

The basic subject of the film is a critique of our civilization, in which frustrated love leads to aggression. Social convention demands that a pair of lovers at a party have to be separated. This makes the man so aggressive that he kicks a dog for no apparent reason and kills a bug in a fit of rage. Twenty years later, Buñuel was to elaborate on the same theme in *Los Olvidados,* a film about the brutalization of youth resulting from lack of love.

The subject of brutality is closely examined in *L'Age d'or:* the members of upper-class society remain quite unmoved when a servant is injured in a fire and when the son of the estate manager is shot over a trifle. What does move them is the slap a host gives to the hostess at a dinner party. Buñuel judges social differences by showing the class-conditioned reactions to various forms of brutality.

"In my opinion," Buñuel said, "a film, besides being a form

53. Luis Buñuel and Salvador Dali. Final scene from the film *Un Chien Andalou*. 1928

of entertainment, must stand for—and indirectly convey—the idea that we live in a brutal, hypocritical, unjust world." A manifesto in the program for *L'Age d'or* contains these remarks: "In these times of so-called prosperity, the social function of *L'Age d'or* must be the encouragement of the masses to quench their thirst for destruction and maybe even the encouragement of masochism in the oppressors." The manifesto is signed by Aragon, Breton, René Char, Crevel, Dali, Eluard, Péret, Tzara, and others.

The film, with its brutal and blasphemous scenes, has such an aggressive effect because it shows, with apparent reasonableness, totally incomprehensible things as if they were self-evident and commonplace, while, at the same time, it shows the commonplace to be incomprehensible.

"For me, bourgeois morality is immorality and I must fight against it. Any morality that is based on our most unjust institutions such as religion, fatherland, family, culture—in short, everything we call the 'pillars of society' " (Buñuel, 1961).

Soon after its premiere in the Studio 28 in Paris, in 1930, the film's performance was interrupted by a group of radical rightists, calling themselves Les Camelots du Roi. They tore apart the theater and destroyed an exhibition connected with the film in the foyer of the building. The exhibition contained works by Dali, Ernst, Miró, and Tanguy. The film had to be withdrawn. There was a rumor that the producers were threatened with excommunication if they did not destroy all existing prints.

The Studio 28 was one of the earliest noncommercial movie theaters. Makers of Surrealist films were dependent on such houses. The very first one had opened in Paris in 1924. In 1926 the Studio des Ursulines was established and then, in 1928, the Studio 28. Finally, in 1929, the Oeil de Paris opened up. These houses mostly showed avant-garde films which also were shown at the first international avant-garde film festival in Berlin in 1925, by the London Film Society in 1929, and were included in the film program of the international exhibition *Film und Foto* that opened in Stuttgart under the auspices of the Deutscher Werkbund (1929).

The Situation Between 1930 and 1939—"The Independence of Art on the Side of the Revolution"

The second Surrealist manifesto, which Breton published in 1929 in the final number of *La Révolution surréaliste*, contains, among other things, long paragraphs in which former members of the movement and many sympathizers are covered with invective: Artaud and Masson, Soupault, Desnos, and Picabia. The men thus attacked published a pamphlet of their own, attacking Breton. They used the same title which, a few years earlier, had been given to an essay against Anatole France: *Un Cadavre*. In it, Breton is called a policeman, a priest, a phony revolutionary, and a pseudo-Communist. The nucleus of the Surrealist group—as shown in a photograph taken by Man Ray in 1930—included Arp, Breton, Crevel, Dali, Eluard, and Ernst, as well as Man Ray, Tanguy, and Tzara, who had been reinstated.

The controversy continued to center on the question whether the Surrealists should involve themselves politically. It was time for a decision; the fascist forces in Europe were becoming more powerful every day. Common action was urgently needed. After much indecision, Breton came out in favor of Communism. The title of his new magazine, which appeared from 1930 to 1933, is characteristic of the change in emphasis: *Le Surréalisme au service de la révolution*. There was no more talk of a Surrealist, spiritual revolution. Surrealism was being placed at the service of the proletarian revolution. The first issue of the new magazine contains an exchange of telegrams with Moscow. One telegram, an inquiry from the Russian International Bureau for Revolutionary Literature, asked how the Surrealists would react if the imperialists declared war on the Soviet Union. The answer was: "Comrades, if imperialism were to declare war on the Soviet Union, we will act according to the directives of the Third International, the same as the members of the French Communist Party" (bibl. 39).

While most Surrealists, and especially Aragon, firmly allied themselves with the Communist Party and shared its revolutionary ideas, Dali stuck to his own highly individualistic painting and let it be known, now and then at least, that he did not dislike Hitler. Although this may well have been a simple case of Surrealist provocation—such differences as those that existed between Aragon and Dali would certainly have produced a split in the Surrealist group if Breton had not held the divergent factions together with a strong hand.

Aragon took part in the Second International Congress of Revolutionary Writers in Kharkov in 1930. Upon his return he proclaimed in the new Surrealist magazine: "The further development of Surrealism must consist of the recognition and unconditional adoption of dialectical materialism as the only revolutionary philosophy by those intellectuals who hitherto have stood for a purely idealistic kind of opposition, if their opposition is to be consistent with the concrete problems of the revolution." At about the same time, Aragon published the poem "Front Rouge" in the magazine *La Littérature de la révolution mondiale,* the organ of the International Union of Revolutionary Writers. The publication of the poem in France resulted in his being accused of inciting to murder. Breton came to Aragon's defense, but Aragon objected to Breton's attacks on the Communist Party and left the Surrealist group. The Surrealists deplored this step, which they did not regard as a political act but as treason against their group. Aragon was branded an opportunist, and the label stuck.

In 1933, Breton, Eluard, and Crevel were expelled from the French Communist Party because of their nonconformist behavior. A short time later, when France was in danger from antiparliamentarian, radical rightist organizations—which drew strength and encouragement from their German neighbors—the three nonconformists called for the establishment of an antifascist action group that was to include all labor organizations. Their proclamation was signed by Fernand Léger, André Lhote, André Malraux, and Paul Signac, among others. On July 27, 1934, the Central Committee of the Communist Party and the leaders of the Socialist Party signed a pact devoted to a common fight against war and fascism.

54. Max Ernst. *Loplop Introduces the Surrealists.* 1931. Collage

Apparently, the ill-fated refusal of the German Communists to ally themselves with the Social Democrats against Hitler had made an impression on both Communists and Socialists in France.

In 1935 there was a writer's congress for the defense of civilization in Paris. The Surrealists were not invited, but Eluard got permission to read a paper which Breton had written. In it, Breton advocated the recent rapprochement between France and Russia for the purpose of keeping fascism at bay. But he also criticized Stalin's repression of public opinion, and quoted from Lenin (1905): "Everyone is free to say and to write whatever he pleases; freedom of the press must remain unimpeded."

Breton considered anything else reactionary. "Whether we move in the realm of politics or of art, there are always these two forces: the refusal to accept conditions as they are and the irresistible need to change them on the one hand; on the other hand, there must be lasting loyalty to the moral precepts that have stood for progress. No one can suppress these forces for years, or fight against them in the name of a messianic idea of what the Soviet Union is doing" (Breton, *Du Temps que les surréalistes avaient raison,* 1935). The pamphlet sums up the experiences had during the congress and ends with this remark: "We can only express our formal mistrust of this regime (in the U.S.S.R.) and of its leader." The pamphlet is signed by Breton, Dali, Dominguez, Eluard, Ernst, Magritte, Oppenheim, Péret, Man Ray, and Tanguy, among others.

Now the break with the Soviet Union was official. Lenin and Trotsky had become the heroes of the movement, not Stalin. A Militant Federation of Revolutionary Intellectuals was founded in 1935 by a group that included Breton, Eluard, Péret, and Roger Blin. It was called Contre-attaque, and its aim was the class struggle and the nationalization of the means of production. But, not being rooted in the proletariat, it foundered rather fast. Still, at that period the political consciousness of the Surrealists was more definitely developed than at any time before. The fact that they refused to accept the Communist doctrines of the 1930s shows their clear-eyed approach to politics. But it also contributed to their isolation and ineffectiveness.

Political and artistic activities went hand in hand. In 1935, there was a "systematic cycle of lectures about the newest ideas of Surrealism" which recalled the big, rowdy affairs of the twenties. Surrealist groups sprang up outside France. And the French group gained new members, including Hans Bellmer, Victor Brauner, Oscar Dominguez, Matta, Richard Oelze, Méret Oppenheim, Wolfgang Paalen, and Kurt Seligmann. There were Surrealist exhibitions at the Galerie Pierre Colle in Paris in 1933; in the Kunsthaus, Zurich, in 1934; at The Museum of Modern Art, New York, in 1936; at the New Burlington Galleries, London, in 1938; and in the Galerie des Beaux-Arts in Paris, 1938. Also in 1938, the collected works of Lautréamont were published, with illustrations by Brauner, Dominguez, Ernst, Magritte, Man Ray, Masson, Matta, Miró, Paalen, Seligmann, and Tanguy. After *Le Surréalisme au service de la révolution* stopped publication, the Surrealists contributed mainly to the Skira-Tériade periodical *Minotaure.* In the graphic arts, new methods of picture-making were developed: Wolfgang Paalen's *fumage* (fig.

55. Man Ray. Montage of portrait photographs. Left to right: Breton, Ernst, Dali, Arp; Tanguy, Char, Crevel, Eluard; De Chirico, Giacometti, Tzara, Picasso; Magritte, Brauner, Péret, Rosey; Miró, Mesens, Hugnet, Man Ray. 1934

59), Oscar Dominguez's decalcomania (fig. 57). Bellmer, Dali, Dominguez, Ernst, Wilhelm Freddie, Maurice Henry, Miró, Oppenheim (fig. 60), and Kurt Seligmann concentrated some of their attention on the creation of objects in the tradition of Duchamp and Dada. The exhibition at the Galerie des Beaux-Arts, which the Surrealists staged with Duchamp's cooperation in 1938, turned into a total environment made up of antiart objects (figs. 65–68).

That same year, Breton went on a trip to Mexico, where he met Trotsky at the house of Diego Rivera. The result was a manifesto that proved to be of great importance, for both Trotsky and Breton. Communist and Surrealist met on the common ground of their reaction to Stalinism and their interest in the revolutionary function of art.

Under the heading "Pour un art révolutionnaire indépendant," we read: "We need not explain that at no time—no matter how favorable—do we feel any solidarity with the slogan 'Neither Fascism nor Communism!'—a slogan for conservative and frightened philistines clinging to the remnants of a 'democratic' past. True art, art that does not rely on producing variations of already existing models but tries to express the innermost needs of man today . . . such art must be revolutionary; it must be aimed at a complete and radical revision of the social order."

57. Oscar Dominguez. *Decalcomania.* 1937. Gouache

Trotsky, who was probably the main author of the text, was interested mainly in the intellectual revolutionary potential of art, on the presumption that only a social revolution can make a fundamental change in society and culture. It is interesting to note that Trotsky was inclined to recognize the autonomy of the cultural superstructure: "The artistic opposition today is one of those forces than can contribute ef-

56. Victor Brauner. *Self-Portrait.* 1931. Oil on wood

58. Méret Oppenheim. *La Nuit.* 1934

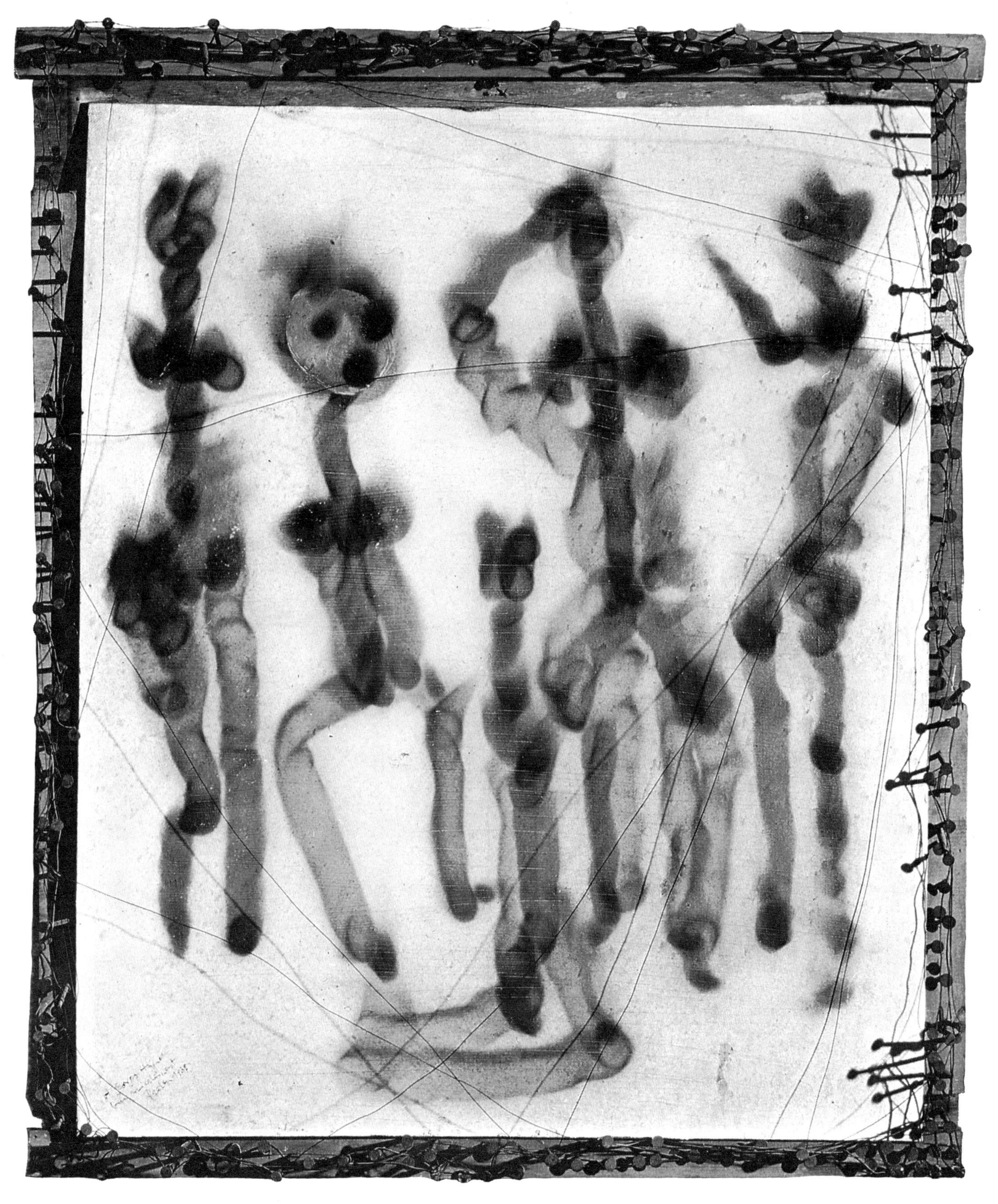

59. Wolfgang Paalen. *Untitled*. 1937. *Fumage*

60. Méret Oppenheim. *Fur-Covered Cup, Saucer, and Spoon.* 1936

fectively to the defeat of a regime that has destroyed all sense of human greatness and dignity—along with the right of the exploited class to strive for a better world."

Together, Breton and Trotsky attacked Stalinist indoctrination: "Free choice . . . [of] subject matter and absolute freedom of research are rights which the artist justly considers inalienable. In matters of art it is essential that imagination be completely free from coercion, that no pressure of authority be exerted on it . . . in art, all is permitted."

On the political function of art they stated: "All that has been said here clearly shows that our defense of freedom of the arts is not an attempt at justification of political indifference, and that we are far from wanting to resurrect a so-called pure art which usually serves the most impure purposes of reaction. No, our idea of the function of art is too lofty to deny its influence on the destiny of society. We regard it as the noblest task of art to work consciously and actively toward revolution."

The pamphlet was "to find a basis on which revolution-

61. Méret Oppenheim. From *A Pupil's Notebook.* 1931–32

ary artists could unite in order to serve the revolution and defend the freedom of art, even against those who have usurped the revolution." Since the fascists had branded all progressive art as degenerate, and Stalinism had branded all free art as fascist, it was up to the revolutionary artists to engage in a common struggle against persecution by all reactionary forces. In order to accomplish this, a Federation Internationale de l'Art Révolutionnaire Indépendant was to be founded. Its aim: "Freedom of art—for the revolution. Revolution—for the ultimate freedom of art."

Returning to Paris, Breton founded a French branch of this federation. Among its members were Yves Allégret, Jean Giono, Pierre Mabille, and André Masson. Eluard did not join because, during the controversy over Stalinism, he had gone from the Surrealist to the Communist camp. When Breton called for a boycott against Eluard, Ernst left the Surrealists, in protest. The monthly magazine published by the new federation was called *Clé*. It appeared twice, until the avalanche of political events made further publication impossible.

In 1939, Matta and Tanguy emigrated to the United States. Paalen fled to Mexico. Miró went back to Spain. In 1940, Brauner disappeared in Switzerland. Dali and Man Ray arrived in the United States. Péret, imprisoned for having taken part in the Spanish Civil War, managed to escape. By 1941, he was in the United States, as were Breton, Wifredo Lam, Masson, and Seligmann. Ernst was imprisoned repeatedly, but finally he succeeded, with Peggy Guggenheim's help, to get to the United States, where he arrived in 1941. Desnos and Eluard stayed in France and worked in the Resistance.

Once again the pressure of the political situation created a turning point in the course of Surrealism. Back in 1925, the war in Morocco had stirred up political controversy within the group, resulting in an emphatic left-wing engagement. In

62. Man Ray. *The Enigma of Isidore Ducasse.* 1920. Cloth and rope over sewing machine

the early thirties, the rapid rise of fascism had brought about a rapprochement between the Surrealists and Communism; but Stalinism had put an end to this and had led to the 1938 manifesto by Trotsky and Breton. During the Spanish Civil War, Max Ernst, Masson, Matta, Miró, Péret, and others were on the side of the Republicans. Now, the outbreak of World War II broke up the group and the movement came to an end. Its members had more or less gone their own way starting in the thirties, each pursuing his own artistic development. This individualization had taken place despite much talk about the need for common political action and group unity. We need only consider Miró's abstract pictures, Masson's caricature-like drawings, Dali's self-canonizations, Tanguy's stereotypification.

Surrealism in Exile

In New York, where Chagall, Léger, Lipchitz, Mondrian, and other European artists had by now established themselves, the Surrealists did not have an easy time. "There were artists in New York, but there was no art. One man alone cannot make art. It depends too much on an exchange of ideas with others. . . . We were so isolated that we had to start from zero, as it were" (Ernst). Still, Surrealism had created some interest in the United States during the ten preceding years. In 1931, the first important Surrealist exhibition had taken place in Hartford, Connecticut. That same year, Ernst had a show in New York. From 1934 on, the Julien Levy Gallery there showed works by Dali, Giacometti, Arp, Masson, Miró, and Man Ray. In 1936 Julien Levy published, in New York, an anthology of Surrealism. The same year The Museum of Modern Art presented *Fantastic Art, Dada and Surrealism*. Then there were, from 1941 on, such focal points as the Pierre Matisse Gallery, Peggy Guggenheim's gallery Art of This Century (designed by Frederick Kiesler in 1942), and the magazine *View*, which Charles Henri Ford had founded in 1940 and which devoted a special issue in 1941 to Sur-

63. Hans Bellmer. *The Doll.* 1934

64. Hans Bellmer. *Balljointparasollighter.* 1938

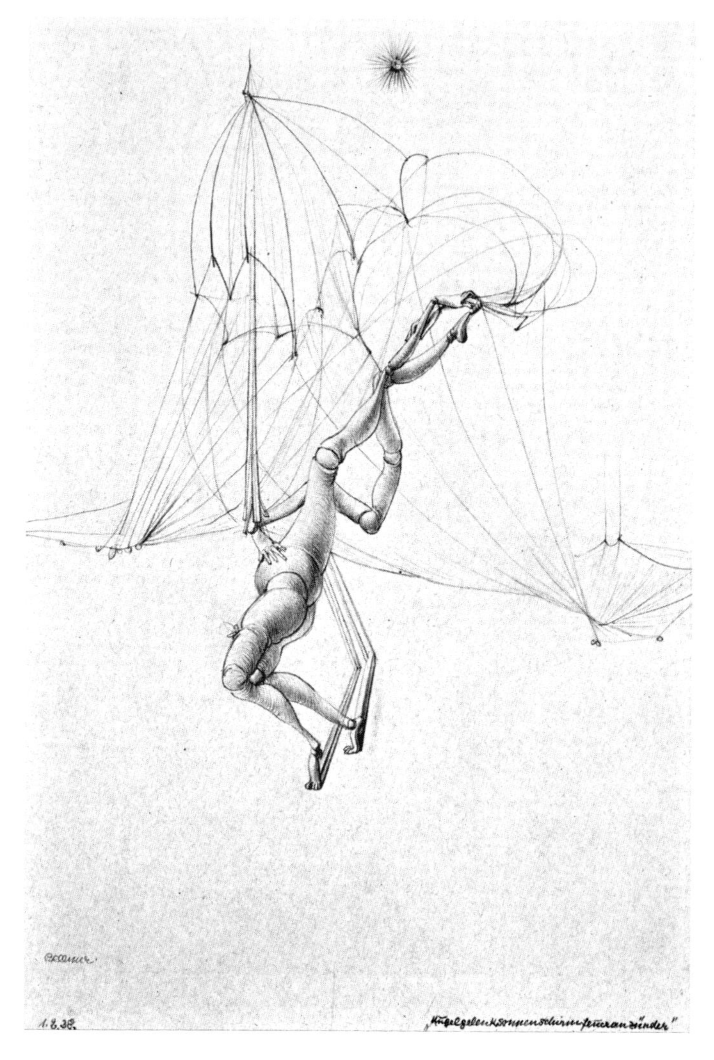

65–68. International Exhibition of Surrealism in Paris (Galerie des Beaux-Arts), 1938. Objects: Salvador Dali, *Window Dummy* and *Rainy Taxi*; Kurt Seligmann, *Cage for the Hands of Will-o'-the-Wisps;* André Masson, *Pensée*

realism. In subsequent issues, Max Ernst, Duchamp, and Tanguy were discussed. In 1942 David Hare, Breton, and Max Ernst established the magazine *VVV,* to which Robert Motherwell, Harold Rosenberg, and William Carlos Williams contributed. The first issue contains Breton's "Prolegomena to a Third Surrealist Manifesto or Else" (1942), the second has Breton's "Situation du Surréalisme entre les deux guerres" (1943).

In 1942 the Surrealists presented themselves to the American art public in a single, large group exhibition in the Whitelaw Reid mansion on Madison Avenue in New York. Alongside works by Arp, Bellmer, Brauner, Duchamp, Max

69. Wifredo Lam. *Mother and Child.* 1942

Ernst, Giacometti, Lam, Matta, Magritte, Miró, Masson, Oelze, Picasso, and Seligmann, the show contained works by Baziotes, Calder, Jimmy Ernst, Hare, Kiesler, Klee, Moore, and Motherwell. The catalogue, designed by Duchamp, was called *First Papers of Surrealism*—an allusion to the First Papers of naturalization. The preface was written by Sidney Janis.

The center of modern art had moved from Paris to New York. Among the other artists who had come to the United States were Josef Albers, Lyonel Feininger, László Moholy-Nagy, Hans Hofmann, Naum Gabo, Walter Gropius, Marcel Breuer, and Mies van der Rohe. Not since the 1913 Armory Show had America received so strong an influx from Europe. While the teachings of such artists as Albers and Hofmann were of fundamental importance for a whole new generation of American artists, the Surrealists exerted a strong influence on artists such as Arshile Gorky, Robert Motherwell, and Jackson Pollock. True to the character of Surrealism, this influence has nothing to do with style, but with those quasi-automatic production methods which, in turn, led to the development of a specifically American style: Action Painting. The most obvious example of this is the story, abbreviated into a legend, of how Jackson Pollock discovered Max Ernst's new oscillation technique in 1942: "Tie an empty can to a string approximately 2 feet long, make a small hole in the bottom of the can and fill it with liquid paint. Let the can swing back and forth over a horizontal canvas; guide it by moving your hands, arms, shoulder, entire body. In this way, surprising lines will drop onto the canvas. Then, the game of mental associations can begin." Ernst reports that this is the way he instructed the young American painters in his oscillation technique. Of course, it would be simplistic to ascribe the transition from the semiautomatic work of the Surrealists to American Action Painting to one such isolated incident. But, by the time New York artists became acquainted with the work of the Surrealists, they were ready to look on psychic-inspirative methods and especially on the drip methods as particularly suitable to their own creative strivings.

Now that Surrealism was beginning to pass into the hands of a new generation, there were new principles, new goals. The active phase of Surrealism in Europe was finished. In the forties and fifties we hear more about Motherwell, Gorky, Pollock, Willem de Kooning, Clyfford Still, and Mark Rothko than about Dali, Max Ernst, Magritte, or Tanguy. At that crucial period, Matta and Lam were creative intermediaries between the European artists and their American colleagues.

After the end of World War II, many artists went back to Paris, where those who had worked in the Resistance played a leading role. In 1947 Tzara lectured on "Le Surréalisme et l'après-guerre" and demanded that the Surrealists unite with the Communists in the name of *art engagé*. Breton protested.

Somewhat later, Jean-Paul Sartre published an article in which he took Surrealism to task for being politically abstract, metaphysical, and unrealistic (in *Les Temps modernes*, Paris, 1947). He accused the Surrealists of having been incapable of political action when the situation called for it. The Surrealists counterattacked with a manifesto,

70. Arshile Gorky. *The Diary of a Seducer.* 1945. Oil on canvas

71. Matta. *The Horbits of Patricia.* 1940

"Rupture inaugurale" (1947), simultaneously declaring their distrust of the Communist Party. There was no end to the controversy. Discussions, arguments, recriminations, exclusions continued. But the fifties saw the first retrospectives, proof that Surrealism had become history. In 1970, a new wave of rediscovery began, based on a knowledge of the movement's origin and development.

What has survived into the present is a set of Surrealist principles: the rapprochement of art to reality; the disruption of established values and modes of behavior; the artlessness in art. The work of such artists as Allan Kaprow, John Cage, Jean Dubuffet, Jean Tinguely, Yves Klein, Piero Manzoni, Richard Hamilton, and Andy Warhol would be unthinkable without the seminal influence of Surrealism. The paintings, objects, and films of the Surrealists may have entered the pages of art history, but their ideas keep coming back in ever new guises.

CHRONOLOGY

1924
André Breton publishes his first Surrealist manifesto in Paris. The magazine *La Révolution surréaliste* is founded. Louis Aragon, René Crevel, Robert Desnos, Paul Eluard, Max Morise, Pierre Naville, Benjamin Péret, and Philippe Soupault are members of the movement, as are Max Ernst, André Masson, and Joan Miró, but not Francis Picabia and Tristan Tzara. A Bureau de Recherches Surréalistes is established in Paris. Automatic drawing and writing are introduced. Masson has his first one-man show at the Galerie Simon in Paris. Ivan Goll publishes the first and only issue of the magazine *Surréalisme;* Aragon publishes *Une Vague de réves* (automatic texts). Other publications are: *Les Pas perdus* by Breton; "Detours" by Crevel; "Mourir de ne pas mourir" by Eluard; "Les Reines de la main gauche" by Naville; "Immortelle Maladie" by Péret.

1925
There is political controversy, brought on by the war in Morocco, about the goal of Surrealism. Tanguy and Prévert join the Surrealists; Hans Arp is a member; Pierre Roy is closely aligned to Surrealism. Creation of the *cadavre exquis.* Max Ernst develops *frottage.* The Galerie Pierre in Paris shows *La Peinture surréaliste* with works by Arp, De Chirico, Ernst, Klee, Masson, Miró, Picasso, Man Ray, Pierre Roy; the first showing of Miró's Surrealist pictures is at the Galerie Pierre.

1926
The Galerie Surréaliste opens in Paris, with works by Man Ray. Miró and Max Ernst design stage sets for Diaghilev's Ballets Russes. There is a Marxist attack on the Surrealists in Naville's essay "La Révolution et les intellectuels." Breton counters with *Légitime défense.* Naville leaves the ranks of the Surrealists; Antonin Artaud and Philippe Soupault are expelled. Marc Allégret, Duchamp, and Man Ray make the film *Anemic Cinema.* Publications: Max Ernst, *Histoire naturelle* (*frottages*); Aragon, "Le Paysan de Paris"; Crevel, "La Mort difficile"; Eluard, "Capitale de la douleur."

1927
One-man shows by Ernst (Galerie Van Leer, Paris), Tanguy (Galerie Surréaliste, Paris), and Magritte (Galerie Le Centaur, Brussels). Magritte, attracted by the Surrealists, moves to Le Perreux-sur-Marne near Paris for three years. Man Ray produces the film *Emak Bakia;* Germaine Dulac and Artaud make the film *La Coquille et le clergyman.* Breton publishes *Introduction au discours sur le peu de réalité* (about Surrealist objects).

1928
Dali comes to Paris and joins the Surrealists. Surrealist exhibition at the Galerie Au Sacre du Printemps, with works by Arp, De Chirico, Ernst, Georges Malkine, Masson, Miró, Picabia, Roy, and Tanguy; De Chirico exhibition in the Galerie Surréaliste; Miró exhibition in the Galerie Georges Bernheim. Man Ray and Desnos make the film *L'Etoile de mer;* Buñuel (with Dali) produces *Un Chien Andalou.* Publications: Breton, *Nadja* and *Le Surréalisme et la peinture;* Eluard, "Defense de savoir"; Péret, "Le Grand Jeu."

72. Jean Arp. *Configuration.* 1928

1929
The final issue of *La Révolution surréaliste,* containing Breton's second Surrealist manifesto, is published. Desnos, Miró, Masson, and Prévert leave the Surrealist group; Alberto Giacometti, Dali, Buñuel, René Char, and Tzara join it. Dali's first one-man show at the Galerie Goemans in Paris. Man Ray produces *Les Mystêres du château de dé.* A special issue of the Belgian magazine *Variétés* is devoted to Surrealism. Max Ernst publishes *La Femme 100 têtes.*

1930
First issue of the magazine *Le Surréalisme au service de la révolution,* containing a declaration of solidarity by Aragon, Buñuel, Dali, Eluard, Ernst, Péret, Tanguy, Tzara, and others with Breton, who had been attacked by renegade and excluded Surrealists. Aragon takes part in the Second International Congress of Revolutionary Writers in Kharkov. Exhibition of collages in the Galerie Goemans in Paris. Buñuel and Dali make the film *L'Age d'or.* Riots incited by radical rightists at the Studio 28 in Paris. Publications: Aragon, "La Peinture au défi"; Dali, *La Femme visible;* Max Ernst, *Rêve d'une petite fille qui voulut entrer au Carmel.*

1931
The first big Surrealist exhibition in the United States, at the Wadsworth Atheneum, Hartford, Conn., with works by De Chirico, Dali, Ernst, Masson, Miró, and Picasso. Crevel publishes *Dali; ou l'Anti-obscurantisme.*

1932
Aragon breaks with the Surrealists; Maurice Henry, Georges Hugnet, Marcel Jean, Méret Oppenheim join the Surrealists. Oelze arrives in Paris. The first one-man show of works by Giacometti is held at the Galerie Pierre Colle in Paris. Breton publishes *Les Vases communicants.* Surrealist exhibition at the Julien Levy Gallery, New York (previously shown at the Wadsworth Atheneum).

1933
Exposition Surréaliste at the Galerie Pierre Colle in Paris, with works by Dali, Duchamp, Eluard, Ernst, Giacometti, Marcel Jean, Magritte, Miró, Picasso, Man Ray, Tanguy, and others. Victor Brauner joins the group. Group show of Surrealist work at the Salon des Surindépendants contains works by Arp, Brauner, Dali, Ernst, Giacometti, Valentine Hugo, Magritte, Miró, Oppenheim, Man Ray, Tanguy, and others. The magazine *Le Surréalisme au service de la révolution* ends publication. Founding of the magazine *Minotaure,* to which several Surrealists contribute. Breton, Eluard, and Crevel are expelled from the French Communist Party.

1934
Oscar Dominguez joins the Surrealists; Richard Oelze makes contact with the group. Dali is taken to task for his interest in the Nazis. Exhibition *Was ist Surrealismus?* in the Kunsthaus, Zurich, contains works by Arp, Ernst, Giacometti, Julio Gonzáles, Miró. One-man shows of Dali and Giacometti at the Julien Levy Gallery, New York. Victor Brauner exhibits at the Galerie Pierre in Paris. Exhibition in the Palais des Beaux-Arts, Brussels, with works by De Chirico, Dali,

73. Pablo Picasso. *Composition.* 1933. Watercolor

Delvaux. Photographs of Bellmer's first *Doll* appear in *Minotaure.* Max Ernst spends the summer with Giacometti in Switzerland and begins a series of sculptures. Publications: Breton, *Qu'est-ce que le Surréalisme?;* Max Ernst, *Une Semaine de bonté;* Eluard, "La Rose publique."

1935
World congress of Writers for the Defense of Culture, in Paris; new controversy over the relationship of Surrealism to Communism. Several Surrealists take part in the Contre-attaque movement, an antifascist Militant Federation of Revolutionary Intellectuals. Wolfgang Paalen and Hans Bellmer join the Surrealists; Giacometti is expelled. Dominguez develops decalcomania. Picasso writes Surrealist poems, using automatic writing. Masson exhibition at the Pierre Matisse Gallery, New York. The first books on Surrealism appear in New York (by James Thrall Soby) and London (by David Gascoyne). Breton publishes *Du Temps que les surréalistes avaient raison;* Dali publishes *La Conquête de l'irrationel.*

1936
Exhibition *Fantastic Art, Dada and Surrealism* at The Museum of Modern Art, New York. Exhibition of Surrealist objects at the Galerie Charles Ratton, Paris. *International Surrealist Exhibition* at the New Burlington Galleries, London. Delvaux joins the Belgian Surrealist circle around Magritte and Mesens. The Surrealists in Paris protest the Moscow trials.

1937
Kurt Seligmann and Masson (again) join the movement. Breton opens the Surrealist Galerie Gradiva in Paris. Max Ernst designs stage sets for a Paris production of Alfred Jarry's *Ubu enchaîné;* the program booklet contains a tribute to Jarry with texts and illustrations by Magritte, Miró, Paalen, and Picasso. Paalen develops *fumage.* Breton publishes *L'Amour fou.* Matta joins the Surrealists.

1938
Breton and Trotsky meet in Mexico. They jointly publish the manifesto *Pour un art révolutionnaire indépendant.* International Surrealist Exhibition at the Galerie des Beaux-Arts in Paris (directors: Breton, Eluard, Duchamp). The *Dictionnaire abrégé du Surréalisme* is published. Bellmer moves to Paris. Eluard leaves the Surrealists and becomes a Communist. Max Ernst counters Breton's call for a boycott by resigning from the Surrealist group in sympathy with Eluard. Wifredo Lam arrives in Paris and makes friends with the Surrealists; his works are exhibited at the Galerie Pierre. The collected works of Lautréamont are published in Paris and are illustrated by Brauner, Dominguez, Ernst, Magritte, Man Ray, Masson, Matta, Miró, Paalen, Seligmann, and Tanguy.

1939
Matta and Tanguy emigrate to the United States; Paalen flees to Mexico; Miró returns to Spain. Breton and Péret are drafted into the French army. Max Ernst is imprisoned.

1940
Brauner goes to Switzerland. Dali and Man Ray arrive in the United States. Breton, released from military service, goes to Marseilles, from where he hopes to flee the country. Matta exhibition at the Julien Levy Gallery, New York.

1941
Breton, Ernst, Lam (later in Santo Domingo), Masson, Péret (later in Mexico), and Seligmann emigrate to the United States. Miró and Dali exhibitions at The Museum of Modern Art, New York. The American magazine *View* devotes a special issue to the Surrealist movement. Robert Motherwell makes contact with the Surrealists-in-exile.

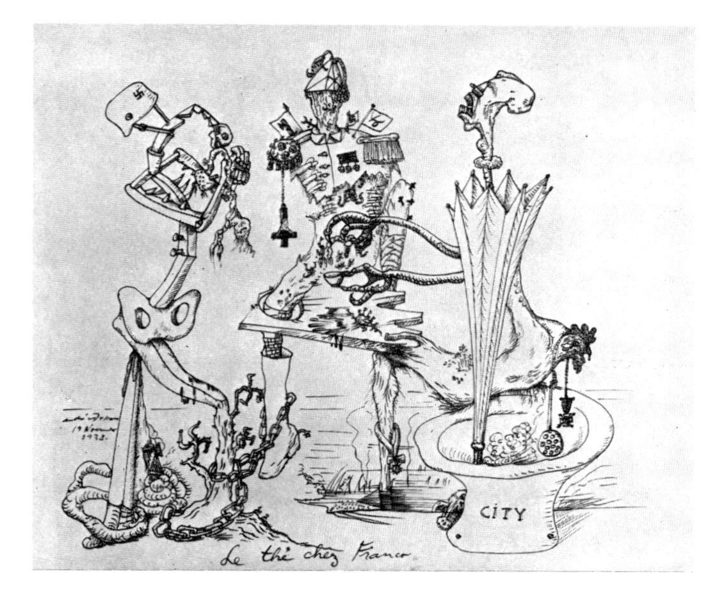

74. André Masson. *Tea at Franco's.* 1938

1942
Exhibition *Artists in Exile* at the Pierre Matisse Gallery, New York. The magazine *VVV* is fcunded by David Hare, Breton, and Ernst. The first issue contains Breton's "Prolegomena to a Third Surrealist Manifesto or Else." Exhibition *First Papers of Surrealism* at 451 Madison Avenue, New York, in which young American artists join the Surrealists. Ernst develops the oscillation technique. Special issues of the magazine *View* devoted to Max Ernst and Yves Tanguy. Dali publishes *The Secret Life of Salvador Dali.*

1943
Breton publishes "Situation du surréalisme entre les deux guerres" in *VVV.* Pollock exhibition in Peggy Guggenheim's gallery, Art of This Century, New York.

1944
Baziotes and Motherwell have their first one-man shows in the gallery Art of This Century, New York. Breton sponsors Arshile Gorky.

1945
Exhibitions of Mark Rothko (Art of This Century) and Gorky (Julien Levy Gallery) in New York. A special issue of *View* devoted to Duchamp. Brauner and Masson return to Paris. Desnos dies in Terezin concentration camp. First volume of Maurice Nadeau's *Histoire du Surréalisme* is published.

1946
Breton and Arp return to Paris.

1947
International Surrealist exhibitions in Chicago (Art Institute) and Paris (Galerie Maeght). The Maeght exhibition, organized by Breton and Duchamp, is the last important show staged by members of the movement. Disagreements between Breton on one side, and Tzara and Jean-Paul Sartre on the other, about the political relevance of Surrealism.

1948
Artaud dies. Gorky commits suicide. Brauner and Matta are expelled.

1951
First Max Ernst retrospective in Brühl, near Cologne.

1952
Death of Eluard. Paalen returns to Paris. Surrealist exhibition in Saarbrücken.

1953
Max Ernst returns to Paris. Tanguy is expelled.

1954
Max Ernst is expelled.

1955
Giacometti retrospective at The Solomon R. Guggenheim Museum, New York; De Chirico retrospective at The Museum of Modern Art, New York. Tanguy dies.

1957
Dominguez commits suicide.

1959
Paalen commits suicide. Surrealist exhibition at the Galerie Daniel Cordier, Paris. Max Ernst retrospective at the Musée National d'Art Moderne, Paris.

1965
Giacometti dies. Retrospectives: Magritte, at The Museum of Modern Art, New York; Dali, at the Gallery of Modern Art, New York; Brauner, at the Museum des 20. Jahrhunderts, Vienna; Oelze at the Kestner-Gesellschaft, Hanover.

1966
Death of Arp, Brauner, Breton. Man Ray retrospective at the Los Angeles County Museum of Art.

1967
Death of Magritte. Retrospectives: Bellmer at the Kestner-Gesellschaft, Hanover; Dominguez at the Städtisches Museum, Leverkusen, Germany; Oppenheim at the Moderna Museet, Stockholm; Magritte at the Museum Boymans–van Beuningen, Rotterdam.

1968
Exhibition *Dada, Surrealism, and Their Heritage* at The Museum of Modern Art, New York. Masson retrospective at the Musée Cantini, Marseilles.

1970–72
Retrospectives: Giacometti at the Orangerie, Paris; De Chirico at the Palazzo Reale, Milan; Dali at the Museum Boymans–van Beuningen, Rotterdam, and at the Kunsthalle, Baden-Baden; Max Ernst at the Württembergische Kunstverein, Stuttgart; Bellmer at the Centre National d'Art Contemporaine, Paris; Brauner at the Musée National d'Art Moderne, Paris; Man Ray at the Museum Boymans–van Beuningen, Rotterdam.

COLORPLATES

Colorplate 2

GIORGIO DE CHIRICO (b. 1888)

The Return of the Poet

Painted in 1911(?)
Oil on canvas, 34 1/4 × 26"
Private collection

The composition of this picture is simple: two facades, extending into the foreground from either side, flank the scene like the wings of a theater stage. A shadow cast by the structure on the right throws the entire foreground zone into darkness. The bottom of the painting is bordered by a train running parallel to the picture plane. At the back of a middle zone of indefinite depth, and bathed in light, a chimney, a tower, and a small house stand side by side. Still farther back is a third zone, containing the simple outlines of a hilly landscape.

Although the picture has depth, it lacks spatial continuity. The breaks between the different zones make it impossible to gauge distance, and while the architectural elements are shown in individual perspective, the rules of central perspective are ignored. The tower and the house are strongly illumined by a light that seems to come from the right, but the chimney seems to receive far less light. The pennants on the tower indicate that the wind is blowing from the right, but the cloud of steam issuing from the locomotive in the foreground rises perfectly straight in windless air.

These contradictions give the picture a disturbing character—though it is impossible to say precisely what causes the almost imperceptible sense of malaise it conveys. Presumably, De Chirico painted *The Return of the Poet* in Paris in 1911, after a visit to Turin where he had been much impressed by the city's piazzas—and the general layout of the picture does bear an undeniable resemblance to the piazzas of Turin. But the painting is by no means a direct reflection of reality. In his subsequent work, De Chirico repeatedly made use of the same elements—piazzas, arcaded facades, towers, chimneys, and trains. He used them to create a pictorial world which at first appears simple and clear but whose inner contradictions make it mysterious and artificial.

De Chirico was to refer to this separation of objects from their real content as "metaphysical": "Things become metaphysical for me when accurate coloring and precise dimensions make them the opposite of everything that is confused and vague." The picture which thus makes objects seem strange while at the same time placing them in some sort of order constitutes a permanent (De Chirico says "immortal") opposite to the evanescence of reality.

In this painting De Chirico has employed the elements of an illusionist stage setting—facades, horizontal light, and long breaks in spatial continuity. But it is a transparent illusionism, implied rather than fully realized. And this is what gives the picture its traumatic character—especially as it is empty of all human life. Certain aspects of Adlerian individual psychology are included as well: the dynamic contemporaneity of the train, for instance—in harsh juxtaposition with the static quality of the architectural elements—may well represent childhood memories of a longing for distance, for escape.

Giorgio de Chirico was born in Greece in 1888 of Italian parents. His father was an engineer who worked on a railroad in Thessaly. In 1905, after his father's death, De Chirico and his mother moved to Italy and then to Munich, where Arnold Böcklin's paintings and Nietzsche's writing made a profound impression on him. From 1910 he spent over a year in Florence; soon after this he moved to Paris, where he painted those pictures which Apollinaire in 1913 characterized as metaphysical. Towers and city squares are recurring motifs (for instance, *The Great Tower,* 1913; *Nostalgia of the Infinite,* 1913–14; *The Great Tower,* 1914; *The Tower,* c. 1914; *The Enigma of an Autumn Afternoon,* 1910). De Chirico has commented: "My Böcklin period was over, and I began to choose motifs through which I tried to express the powerful, mysterious feeling I had discovered in Nietzsche: the melancholy of a lovely autumn afternoon in an Italian city. It was the prelude to the Piazze d'Italia which I painted somewhat later, in Paris" (*Memorie della mia vita,* 1945).

From 1915 on, De Chirico lived in Ferrara, where he and Carlo Carrà founded the Scuola Metafisica. Toward the end of that decade and under the influence of Renaissance art in Rome, De Chirico turned to a kind of classical style which was not as meaningful to the Surrealists as his early work between 1911 and 1918 had been.

Colorplate 3

GIORGIO DE CHIRICO

The Disquieting Muses

Painted in 1916

Oil on canvas, 38 1/4 × 26"

Collection Gianni Mattioli, Milan

"What will be the aim of painting in the future? . . . The total elimination of man as guide to or means for the expression of symbols, emotions, thought; the ultimate liberation of painting from the kind of anthropomorphism which is also strangling sculpture? Every object, including man, must be seen *as* object. . . . The arcade exists for all times. . . . Its beauty lies in its design: enigma of fate, symbol of inflexible will" (De Chirico, "Meditations of a Painter," 1912). Such mystifying statements are contradicted by others; this must have been especially fascinating to the Surrealists. "In order to be truly immortal, a work of art must transcend the boundaries of the human: there is no room for commonsense and logical thought. . . . A really profound work must come from the depths of the artist's being" ("From an Early Manuscript II," bibl. 85).

Pierre Roy, in 1914, was greatly impressed by De Chirico's pictures. In 1919 Max Ernst discovered reproductions of De Chirico's work—in the magazine *Valori plastici*—which influenced him profoundly: Ernst's *Pietà or Revolution by Night* of 1923 (fig. 15) is a direct reference to De Chirico's *The Child's Brain* of 1914 (fig. 14). Also in 1923, Magritte was fascinated by De Chirico's *The Song of Love* (1914), and Paul Eluard bought several of De Chirico's pictures during the current Biennale in Rome. The same year, a sailor named Yves Tanguy decided to become a painter after happening upon a picture by De Chirico in the window of Paul Guillaume's gallery in Paris. Dali, too, was inspired by reproductions of the proto-Surrealist's works.

That enigmatic combination of incompatible elements which so fascinated the Surrealists is present in *The Disquieting Muses.* A floor of wooden planks supports a stagelike arrangement of figures like statues (the muses), one piece of sculpture (Apollo Musagetes—Apollo, Leader of the Muses), and several quite unclassifiable objects. The plank floor is bordered on the right by an arcade in shadow. In the background are a structure resembling the Castello Estense in Ferrara and a group of houses with two tall smokestacks. These buildings lie below the level of the stage floor, which is raked up toward the back, effecting a break in the continuity of the scene. Shadows diverge that should converge; the brightly painted box in the foreground defies all rules of perspective, broadening rather than narrowing toward the back; a shadow of unexplained origin falls into the picture at the right.

Most important is the introduction of an artificial figure, a mannequin turned sculpture. De Chirico's mannequins may derive from puppets or dressmakers' dummies, but since he often took his inspiration from secondary sources, it is entirely possible that the original source for the mannequins was the central character of Alberto Savinio's (the professional name of De Chirico's brother Andrea) dramatic sketch, *Les Chants de la mi-mort* (The Songs of the Half-Dead). This character has no personality, no face, no eyes, no voice. The playlet—influenced, no doubt, by Alfred Jarry's *Ubu Roi*—was published in Apollinaire's magazine, *Les Soirées de Paris,* in 1914. Savinio has confirmed this surmise regarding the origin of the mannequins.

The mannequins make their first appearance in *The Philosopher and the Poet* (1914). They recur as leading motifs in 1916 and 1917 in *Hector and Andromache* and *The Troubadour,* and later in *The Return of the Prodigal* (1922).

But these mannequins are also quite obviously related to the Antique statues in many of the pictures De Chirico painted during the early part of the decade, for instance in his *Melancholy* of 1912. At first, as in *The Philosopher and the Poet,* the mannequins correspond to the character in Savinio's play, but later, in *The Endless Voyage* (1914) and *The Torment of the Poet* (1914), they definitely hark back to the artist's earlier pictures of Antique statuary. From then on, the mannequins appear in three different forms: humanized, as in *The Troubadour* and *Hector and Andromache;* dehumanized and transformed into monuments constructed of drafting instruments, as in *The Grand Metaphysician;* and re-formed into quasi-Antique statuary, as in *The Disquieting Muses.*

James Thrall Soby's interpretation of the mannequins as son-symbols in the context of estrangement from the father seems confirmed by a 1917 drawing called *The Return* and by several subsequent canvases entitled *The Return of the Prodigal.* And Max Ernst deliberately employs this concept in his own *Pietà* (fig. 15), in which the father from De Chirico's *The Return* sits with a lifeless, statue-like son-figure in his lap.

Some of the mannequin pictures exist in more than one version. In 1924, Eluard wanted to buy the 1917 version of *The Disquieting Muses* from an Italian private collection. When this proved to be too expensive, De Chirico painted a new version which later became part of a private collection in New York. A still later version, dated 1918, may actually have been painted as late as 1948, according to Soby.

G.deChirico

Colorplate 4

MAX ERNST (b. 1891)

The Elephant Celebes

Painted in 1921

Oil on canvas, 49 1/4 × 42 1/2"

Private collection, London

Max Ernst was born in Brühl, Germany, in 1891. He studied philosophy in Bonn before becoming an involuntary participant in World War I—"Max Ernst died on August 1st, 1914. He returned to life on November 11, 1918, a young man who wanted to become a magician and explore the myths of his time" (Ernst). In 1919, he founded the Dada group W/3 in Cologne, together with J. T. Baargeld and Hans Arp. (W stood for Western stupidities, 3 for the three founders.) He helped to publish short-lived polemical magazines and to organize provocative exhibitions in Cologne. In 1921, at Breton's invitation, he showed his latest work in Paris. He wanted to settle there but could not get a resident's visa. Paul and Gala Eluard visited him in Cologne, where he was once again painting large canvases, a practice he had abandoned at the end of his Dada phase. One of the most important of these pictures is the proto-Surrealist *Elephant Celebes,* which was bought by Eluard that same year.

The basic concept derives from De Chirico. Behind a stage floor of undefined depth and texture we see an indication of a low-lying landscape beneath a great expanse of sky. On the stage floor stands a two-legged, kettle-shaped monster with a "neck" and "head," and a "cap" that seems to be made up of De Chirico's drafting instruments. In the right foreground is a headless, lifeless figure (see *The Disquieting Muses,* colorplate 3, where the head of one mannequin lies on the floor). Near the left picture margin stands a slender pole of unexplained purpose or function. Near the right margin, there is a plantlike construction. Through the sky, fish are flying.

The objects are unreal, but the precision with which they are painted gives them the appearance of reality. In the artificial world of the picture, things that do not exist elsewhere become real. The picture constitutes an antiworld of fantasy and the psychic implications of such a world. This is bound to mystify the viewer because—its objective appearance notwithstanding—it is an utterly subjective world.

De Chirico's pictorial world is characterized by abrasive emptiness. *The Elephant Celebes,* on the other hand, conveys an oppressive sense of monstrosity: the huge creature fills the picture in the manner of a portrait head. Both artists turn the world into a place of *things.* Nothing is alive, nothing moves. While the monster is super-dimensional and huge with its bull's head, the shell seems fragile; perhaps it is made of clay. One gains the impression that Max Ernst's chief preoccupation in those years was the relationship between outside and inside, between shell and essence (see *Woman, Old Man, and Flower* of 1923–24, colorplate 5).

In these metaphoric pictures Ernst anticipates the Verism of the Improbable. A few years later, when it was modified by Tanguy, Magritte, Dali, and Roy, Ernst had turned his attention to the use of inspirative techniques and had more or less abandoned the metaphoric pictures so reminiscent of De Chirico.

CELEBES

Colorplate 5

MAX ERNST

Woman, Old Man, and Flower

Painted in 1923–24
Oil on canvas, 38 × 51 1/4"
The Museum of Modern Art, New York City

Two human figures dominate this picture: one, seen in rear view, has a fan-shaped head or headdress, a pierced and hollow cuirass, and arms that are mere outlines. The other figure is an old man with a convex cuplike torso. He holds a small female figure on his arm.

An earlier version, over which this picture was painted, contained, instead of the rear-view figure, another figure with a convex, hollow torso (right foreground) and a creature shaped like a spinning top; the latter motif became the chief subject of a 1924 picture, *Ubu Imperator.*

The old man is a broken clay cup. His hair is long, his hands are large; he has no feet, and his eyes are closed. The openness of the young man's figure contrasts with the old man's introversion. We find this same kind of physical withdrawal from the surrounding world in *Saint Cecilia* (1923).

The cup motif and the transparent body may have metaphysical significance concerning the interrelation of inside and outside, one of Ernst's main themes. In *Saint Cecilia,* the name Cecilia hints at *cécité*—blindness. Later Max Ernst was to say of his *frottages* that they were "a means of getting rid of one's blindness." The visible and the invisible, outside and inside, should interpenetrate each other pictorially, according to the Surrealists. André Breton, in his first Surrealist manifesto (1924), wrote: "I believe in the coming dissolution of these two opposite states of dream and reality into a kind of absolute, a kind—if you like—of superreality [*surréalité*]." Dream and reality, for the Surrealists, are synonymous with inside and outside.

Max Ernst once said that he intended to bring to light the results of "the journeys of discovery into the unconscious" in such a way as to take note of "what one . . . sees, experiences . . . in that border region between the inner and the outer worlds." We find this idea expressed by the nineteenth-century German Romantic painter Caspar David Friedrich, whom Ernst revered: "Close your physical eye so that you may first see your picture with your spiritual eye. Then bring to light what you have seen in the dark, so that it may have its effect on others from the outside in" ("Remarks Made While Contemplating a Collection of Paintings . . . ," c. 1830).

Thus, the invisible, too, must be presented, but directly, not metaphorically-thematically as in *Woman, Old Man, and Flower.* Several Surrealists tried to do just that. Ernst's *Saint Cecilia* plays an invisible instrument; the picture's subtitle is *The Invisible Piano.* In Ernst's Surrealist group portrait, *The Rendezvous of Friends* (1922; frontispiece), René Crevel is seated at an invisible piano. A picture by Magritte painted in 1928 is called *The Flavor of the Invisible.* Dali painted *The Invisible Man* between 1929 and 1933 and *Invisible Harp* in 1934.

The invisible, however, is not identical with dream content. Max Ernst pointed this out in the foreword he contributed to the catalogue of a 1934 exhibition in Zurich, *Was ist Surrealismus?* (What Is Surrealism?). "When we say that the Surrealists are painters of a constantly changing dream reality, we do not mean that they depict their dreams (that would be a kind of descriptive, naive Naturalism) or that each one is building his own little world from dream elements in which to pose benignly or maliciously (that would be flight from time?). It means, rather, that they move freely, boldly, and surely in that physically and psychically real (surreal)—though largely unexplored—border region between inner and outer world. They make note of what they see and experience there and take action whenever their revolutionary instincts suggest it."

weib, greis u. blume

Colorplate 6

MAX ERNST

The Great Forest

Painted in 1927
Oil on canvas, 45 × 57 1/2"
Kunstmuseum, Basel

In 1922, Max Ernst went to Paris, where he continued to move in Dada and Surrealist circles. A profound transformation of his creative work was brought about in 1925 by the development of the *frottage* technique, without which *The Great Forest* would have been unthinkable.

In August of 1925 Ernst spent some time in Pornic, on the coast of Brittany. He was afraid that he might run into difficulties because he had signed—by way of exception—a Surrealist manifesto against the imperialist war France was waging in Morocco. The story of the origin of *frottage* has been often told and need not be repeated here. Suffice it to say that Ernst discovered a way to stimulate his creativity by making rubbings of certain textures and shapes. He did not predetermine or invent his figures but developed them from such shapes in a half-accidental, associative manner—in other words, semiconsciously. In a unique cycle of drawings, soon to be abandoned, Ernst enlarged his pictorial repertoire with the help of the interrelation between a found shape and the imagination it kindled. The artist felt that this was putting him in touch with the "mechanism of poetic inspiration." Breton had called for psychic automatism; Ernst countered with his own dialectic of semiautomatic inspirative technique and intellectual control. A picture was no longer a deliberate invention for Ernst, but a found object risen from the unconscious, which he then reworked consciously, thus putting some distance between his unconscious and his intellect.

The new image thus gained of the artist and his work is one of the most important achievements of Surrealism. Max Ernst himself constantly found new variations for this concept of mutual inspiration and the resulting mystification. He developed new techniques and a tremendous wealth of motifs, especially between the years 1925 and 1940. Those were the years of his Female Portraits, his Bird Monuments, his Hordes and Brides of the Wind, his Earthquakes, Gulf Streams, Fair Seasons, Shellflowers, Inner Faces, Fishbone-Forest, and Forests—a version of which is shown here.

The artist began by applying layers of brick-red and light-green paint in varying thicknesses onto white canvas. In the lower half of the picture—the forest zone—dark brown and black were added with a spatula. Next, the still-wet paint was scraped off with a palette knife—sometimes through several layers—until the inner structure of the forest began to appear. Then the precise outlines of the forest and of the celestial body behind it were added in thick paint with a brush. Finally, the entire picture was worked over and "corrected" with paint and brush.

With these Forest pictures, Max Ernst continued in the German Romantic tradition begun by Friedrich of making the landscape express subjective experience. In his autobiography, Ernst has said of his own childhood: "Mixed feelings the first time he enters a forest, delight and depression. And a feeling which the Romantics have called *Naturgefühl* [nature feeling]. A wonderful elation at being able to breathe freely in the open air, and at the same time an oppressive sense of being imprisoned by hostile trees all around. Outside and inside at the same time, free and imprisoned" (bibl. 93). With their confrontations of dark, impenetrable forest walls and bright rings representing the sun, these pictures are manifestations of the contrast and simultaneity of dark and light, reality and dream, threat and hope.

For Max Ernst, the forest is fraught with both dreamlike memories and trauma. In a prose piece entitled "Les Mystères de la forêt" (1934), he has satirized his own romantic feelings about the forest. The piece deals with the idea of a civilized forest which has lost its mystery and its power to inspire. "Who will be the death of the forests? The day will come when a forest, who had been a skirt-chaser until then, will decide to confine himself to places where no alcohol is served, to tarred roads and Sunday excursions. He will live on stewed newspapers. Weak with virtue, he will forget the bad habits of his youth. He will become geometric, conscientious, dutiful, grammatical, judicious, pastoral, clerical, constructivistic, and republican . . . he will become an associate professor. Will the weather be fine? Of course! We are going hunting with a group of diplomats. . . . Will they praise the forest for its good behavior? I, for one, will not."

The Forest pictures of 1926–27—of which the one shown here is an unusually large example—have as forerunners two collages from the Dada period: *The Little Tear Gland That Says Tic Tac* (1920) and *Forest and Sun* (1920).

Colorplate 7

MAX ERNST

Loplop Introduces a Flower

Painted in 1931

Oil and collage on plywood, 39 × 32''

Collection the artist

About 1930, Max Ernst developed a new character in his pictures which, for two years, became the chief exponent of his pictorial imagination. Derived from his *Anthropomorphic Figures* (1929), this recurring character was dubbed Loplop by Ernst.

Loplop is a mixture of bird (head), easel (body), and human being (legs, sometimes hands). Each of its parts can appear in a number of different ways. Pictures from Ernst's own creative repertoire are presented on the easel: a *frottage,* a collage made from old illustrations, a tangle of plants, a print, one of his own book illustrations, or sometimes a letter, a bill, or a group of Surrealists (fig. 54).

In the example shown here, we see a Shellflower painting and a set of glossy picture prints, the kind that are used for old-fashioned Valentines.

By letting his pictures be presented through an intermediary—his art figure—rather than by himself, Ernst has changed his role, or, better still, he is showing more clearly where he stands in relation to his work. The artist-and-model iconography is adopted and, at the same time, twisted. The artist appears as his own exhibitor and intermediary: he shows his products and thus demonstrates their availability. This seems to indicate a basic change in Ernst's relation toward his artistic activity—a kind of coming into the clear. At forty, he seems to have freed himself from the need to pictorialize oppressive childhood experiences and also from the rules of Surrealism, to the point where he can—with sovereign ease—make his liberating creative work (and thus the creative process itself) his main theme.

The incomparable series of Loplop paintings, drawings, and collages marks a period in Ernst's oeuvre. More than ever before he is preoccupied with his own work, but his brilliant sense of humor keeps him from becoming solemn about it. The reflective process takes place not at the edge of artistic activity but in the picture itself and during the making of the picture.

Similar pictorial résumés by Ernst can be found later, at the beginning of the 1940s, in his Pictures for Young People.

Colorplate 8

MAX ERNST

The Joy of Living

Painted in 1936
Oil on canvas, 28 3/4 × 36 1/4″
Private collection

If, until 1930, art had been a process of self-realization for Max Ernst, it took on a supraindividual character after the Loplop series: it became a critical reflection of his times, his environment, and political developments. The repellent, brainless bird-man monsters of his Barbarian pictures represent the misuse of human power; his *Europe After the Rain* of 1933 and his *Whole Cities* of the same year—which depict destroyed cities, ruined fortresses—are prophetic visions of disaster and destruction. His *Angel of House and Home* (1937) is a horrifying angel of death. It represents both a reaction to the defeat of the Republicans in Spain and a glimpse into the future: "an ironic title for a kind of trampling beast that devastates and destroys everything that stands in its way. This was my impression then of what was going to happen in the world, and I was right" (Ernst, in H. Reinhardt, *Das Selbstportrait,* Hamburg, 1967).

Max Ernst often gave cheerful names to the wrathful pictures he painted in the thirties: *Intimacies* (1935), *Triumph of Love* (1937), *Breakfast in the Grass* (1935–36), *The Nymph Echo* (1936), *Nature in Morning Light* (1936), and, as shown here, *The Joy of Living*. Such sarcastic, deliberately euphemistic titles sometimes refer to famous earlier works. *Breakfast in the Grass* points to Raphael and Manet, *The Joy of Living* to Matisse.

The prototype of the luxuriant jungle whose plants are in the process of turning into animals and monsters might have been Henri Rousseau's *Jungle Landscape with Setting Sun* (1910). In his "cahiers d'art," published in 1937, Ernst himself calls the two animals in the lower half of *The Joy of Living* "demoiselles," referring to certain female insects that devour their partners after the sex act. Similar insects appear in some of Dali's pictures as symbols of castration fear. Ernst seems to be intent on demonstrating that uniting and devouring are the same thing: the creatures in these pictures are not just living in peaceful symbiosis with the plants, but plants and animals seem to devour each other. A variation on this theme can be found in Ernst's Garden Airplane Traps series, painted at the same time. The deceptively idyllic title *The Joy of Living* not only sharply contradicts the content of the actual picture but also makes a stand against the political reality of the period. In returning to his theme of Forest pictures, Ernst was by no means withdrawing into the safety of landscape painting. It was, rather, his way of reacting to the horrors and the cruelties he saw threatening the world—an indirect, enigmatic, and typically artistic form of protest.

Colorplate 9

MAX ERNST

The Robing of the Bride

Painted in 1939

Oil on canvas, 51 × 37 3/4"

Collection Peggy Guggenheim, Venice

Max Ernst's five-volume collage-picture-novel, *Une Semaine de bonté,* was published in Paris in 1934. In this work, wood engravings from popular scientific works, novels, and magazines of the late nineteenth century are used to demonstrate the cramped middle-class world of the late Victorian era. By slightly altering these pictures the artist has turned them into a critical commentary on that world and on the preceding generation. A trivial, melodramatic pictorial situation is turned into a statement with the help of a bit of paste. In order to make his systematic analysis of that parent generation more pointed, Ernst put animal and bird heads on his human figures, as Gustave Doré and J. J. Grandville had done earlier. Thus, using everyday commercial illustrations as source material for his critical cultural analysis, Ernst developed his collage technique into a new kind of pictorial reportage.

In *The Robing of the Bride,* Ernst seems to have had recourse to the possibilities offered by this technique, this time in color. The collage principle has been introduced into the realm of painting. Creatures that are part human and part bird take up almost all the space in a room that calls to mind a Renaissance interior. The creature on the right is more human than bird; the one on the left more bird than human. The one in the center is a human being dressed up as a bird. On one wall of the room, a picture within the picture repeats the essential elements of the scene.

The figures are fantastic inventions. In the headdress of the figure at the right and in the picture within the picture, a new technique has been introduced that was to become extremely important in Ernst's work about 1940: originally invented in 1935 by Oscar Dominguez, the technique is called decalcomania (fig. 57).

The fantastic realism of *The Robing of the Bride* is unusual for Ernst. At that time he was mainly preoccupied with decalcomania for the purpose of metamorphosis, turning random shapes into plants, animals, and other beings, and letting his fantastic creations develop in a playful manner rather than by solemn design.

In 1937, the traveling exhibition *Entartete Kunst* (Degenerate Art), which the Nazi government sent out from Munich, included Ernst's *La Belle Jardinière* of 1923, a work formerly in the Kunstmuseum, Düsseldorf, which is now lost. From 1939 on, Ernst was interned several times by the French as an enemy alien. When the Gestapo came looking for him, he fled to Marseilles, with the help of Peggy Guggenheim, and from there to New York, where he arrived in 1941. He did not return to Europe from the United States until 1953.

Colorplate 10

MAX ERNST

Napoleon in the Wilderness

Painted in 1941
Oil on canvas, 18 1/4 × 15"
The Museum of Modern Art, New York City

Max Ernst's rediscovery of familiar techniques that had not previously been used in art—*frottage, grattage*—had begun to bear fruit within the Surrealist movement when, in the second half of the 1930s, Wolfgang Paalen discovered *fumage* (fig. 59) and Oscar Dominguez developed decalcomania (fig. 57).

André Breton described the technique of decalcomania, which Max Ernst adopted soon afterward: "Spread black gouache of varying thickness on a sheet of glossy white paper with a wide brush, then cover it immediately with a second sheet and press down lightly with the back of your hand. Slowly lift off this second sheet, starting at the upper edge, as if working with a transfer picture, then replace it on the first sheet, then lift it off again until the whole thing is almost completely dry" (bibl. 40).

The shapes produced by this half-mechanical method, just as in Ernst's *frottages,* often reveal themselves as figures which can then be more clearly defined with the brush. The technique of decalcomania, which had been used in rudimentary ways by such men as Victor Hugo, Justinus Kerner, and Koloman Moser, became extremely popular for a while. There are examples by Bellmer, Breton, Marcel Jean, Tanguy, and others.

"Decalcomanie sans objet préconcu" (decalcomania without a preconceived object) is what Dominguez called his technique. The picture is the accidental, if later corrected or completed, result of a purely mechanical process. The artist has no definite aim in mind when he starts out. As in automatic writing and *frottage,* the process of creation and the act of inspiration are more important than the final product.

To judge such works according to stylistic criteria is to misunderstand the intention of the artist. What matters most is not aesthetic appearance but the process of creation: the method. This method is a combination of a semiautomatic print-making process, the development of mysterious forms out of accidental shapes, and the changing of shapes into objects, of objects into other objects (metamorphosis).

What mainly fascinated Max Ernst in decalcomania was, understandably, the interrelation between semiautomatic processes, inspiration, and conscious completion. Having made his first experiments in 1939 with Hans Bellmer while in a detention camp in France, he later elaborated and used this technique in a series of unusually arresting pictures in which female figures, animals, plants, and columns are artfully developed out of indefinite shapes. Max Ernst accomplishes his metamorphoses so smoothly and compellingly that we cannot tell whether dead matter is brought to life in these landscapes or living matter is turned to stone; whether he sees these random shapes primarily as statues or human beings, animals or plants. The ambiguity is intentional. Where Dominguez's decalcomania technique remains flat and unequivocal, Max Ernst used it to create, in the course of several years, a complex and ambivalent pictorial world that remains enigmatic (intentionally so) and shows inspiration of a high order.

Some of these pictures were done in Europe, some after the artist came to the United States. He began *Napoleon in the Wilderness* in France and completed it in Santa Monica, California. The ferocity of his jungle pictures of the thirties has given way to a certain measure of resignation.

Colorplate 11

JOAN MIRO (b. 1893)

The Gentleman

Painted in 1924
Oil on canvas, 20 1/2 × 18"
Kunstmuseum, Basel

Miró was born in Barcelona in 1893. He had gone through a Fauvist phase when, in 1919, while spending some time in Paris, he came under the influence of French Cubism. Simultaneously, he was attracted to the Dadaists, through contact with Tzara, Picabia, Artaud, and Robert Desnos. By 1924, the year of *The Gentleman,* when Surrealism was beginning to establish itself, Miró had become very close to the leaders of that movement—Aragon, Breton, and Eluard. In 1925 he had a one-man show at the Galerie Pierre in Paris, sponsored by Breton. Péret wrote the preface to the catalogue.

During that time, Miró's work underwent a fundamental change. Whereas his earlier paintings had been cultivated and grandly conceived, though with occasional naive touches, he now started out in a new, completely informal manner. Stimulated by Breton's theory of automatism, Miró did automatic drawings and took part in the production of "exquisite corpses." Both methods strongly influenced his new paintings, which might be called the first Surrealist phase of automatic writing. On flat backgrounds, covered with an uneven coat of paint (which sometimes included an early version of the dripping technique), Miró placed words, numbers, and nonobjective and objective shapes. Discarding all principles of composition, spatial organization, and three-dimensional definition—discarding, in short, the entire tradition of French painting—Miró developed quasi-automatic pictures whose most notable characteristic is their playful artlessness. These works do not make a statement about reality; they make a statement about art. The reduction of artistic display and pretension, of forms and colors, to a minimum of significant elements is—in its sketchiness (quite unsuitable to a painting)—a cheerful, witty protest against all grandiose ideas of art. These pictures do not rearrange elements of reality in fantastic new ways; nor do they formulate any program. A work such as *The Gentleman* replaces the reality of a depicted object with the reality of the image itself. By thus becoming autonomous, the image offers entirely new artistic possibilities that defy all artistic convention. This, too, is an important aspect of Surrealist art which is not based on any one principle but on a number of different beginnings.

Breton saw in these pictures by Miró the realization of "pure psychical automatism." But they are not by any means the simple results of unconscious notation. Miró himself once said about his method: "I do not start with the idea that I will paint a certain thing. I start to paint and while I am painting the picture begins to take effect, it reveals itself. In the act of painting, a shape will begin to mean woman, or bird . . . the first stage is free, unconscious." But the second stage, says Miró (and this is very important) is "carefully calculated" (bibl. 121).

XII
Yes.

Colorplate 12

JOAN MIRO

Oh! One of Those Men Who's Done All That

Painted in 1925

Oil on canvas, 51 × 37 1/2"

Collection Aimé Maeght, Paris

In this picture, the principle of artlessness, based on quasi-automatic notation, is taken yet a step further. Where *The Gentleman* still exhibits intentional form, we find here a kind of aimlessness usually associated with graffiti. Informal squiggles are combined with paint smudges and an inscription. Line drawings and calligraphic logograms appear to have been thrown onto the canvas hastily and aimlessly. This arbitrary notation of personal impulses was to find continuity later on, in L'Art Informel; it reappears in contemporary art—for example, in the "artlessness" of Joseph Beuys's drawings. Such works do not try to create new art forms but to show up the absurdity of existing forms.

Miró's *Oh! One of Those Men Who's Done All That,* with its combinations of painting and writing (Miró: "I make no distinction between painting and poetry"), leans upon Max Ernst's picture-poems of 1924 (*Who Is That Very Sick Man?*) which, in turn, are unthinkable without Apollinaire's *calligrammes* of 1913–16. André Breton's poem-objects (fig. 30) are in the same tradition. The Cubists used letters as integral picture elements and as a formal substitute for color. The Surrealists juxtapose and overlay poems and phrases with pictorial forms in order to develop a complex picture language composed of two different mediums.

This complexity has become ambiguity in Miró's picture. First, the text establishes a relationship between *"messieurs"* (writing) and the female figures (picture); second, it appears as if someone, by way of graffiti, had written a comment on a scribble—which makes Miró not the creator of a picture, but a commentator.

But the picture is not a mere sketch. It is a full-size easel painting, and this contrast between minimal content and important medium has an unsettling effect. Its Surrealist elements are the airing of subconscious processes; the enlargement of pictorial possibilities through the principle of artlessness and the combination of writing and drawing; the ambiguity of meaning; and the stance of protest.

Miró's pictures of the middle twenties were included in all Surrealist group exhibitions: at the Galerie Pierre in Paris, in 1925; at the Galerie Au Sacre du Printemps, 1928; at the Studio 28, on the occasion of the first performance of the Dali-Buñuel film *L'Age d'or,* in 1930; at the Wadsworth Atheneum in Hartford, Connecticut, in 1931; at the Kunsthaus, Zurich, in 1934. An article by Breton on Miró appeared in *Le Surréalisme et la peinture,* in 1928. But Miró did not remain part of the nucleus of the Surrealist movement for long; in this respect he resembles most other painters in the group. He had never been one of its dogmatists or theoreticians.

In the years that followed, Miró concentrated more and more on abstract, flat shapes. In ever-varying combination, the elements of an intensely personal picture language became the content of his works. In the course of time, these became set, yet they never lost their delicacy of coloring.

From 1928 on, at the end of Miró's Surrealist phase, his paintings, though fantasy-born, ceased to be fantasy-producing. They lacked those inspirative qualities essential to Surrealist art.

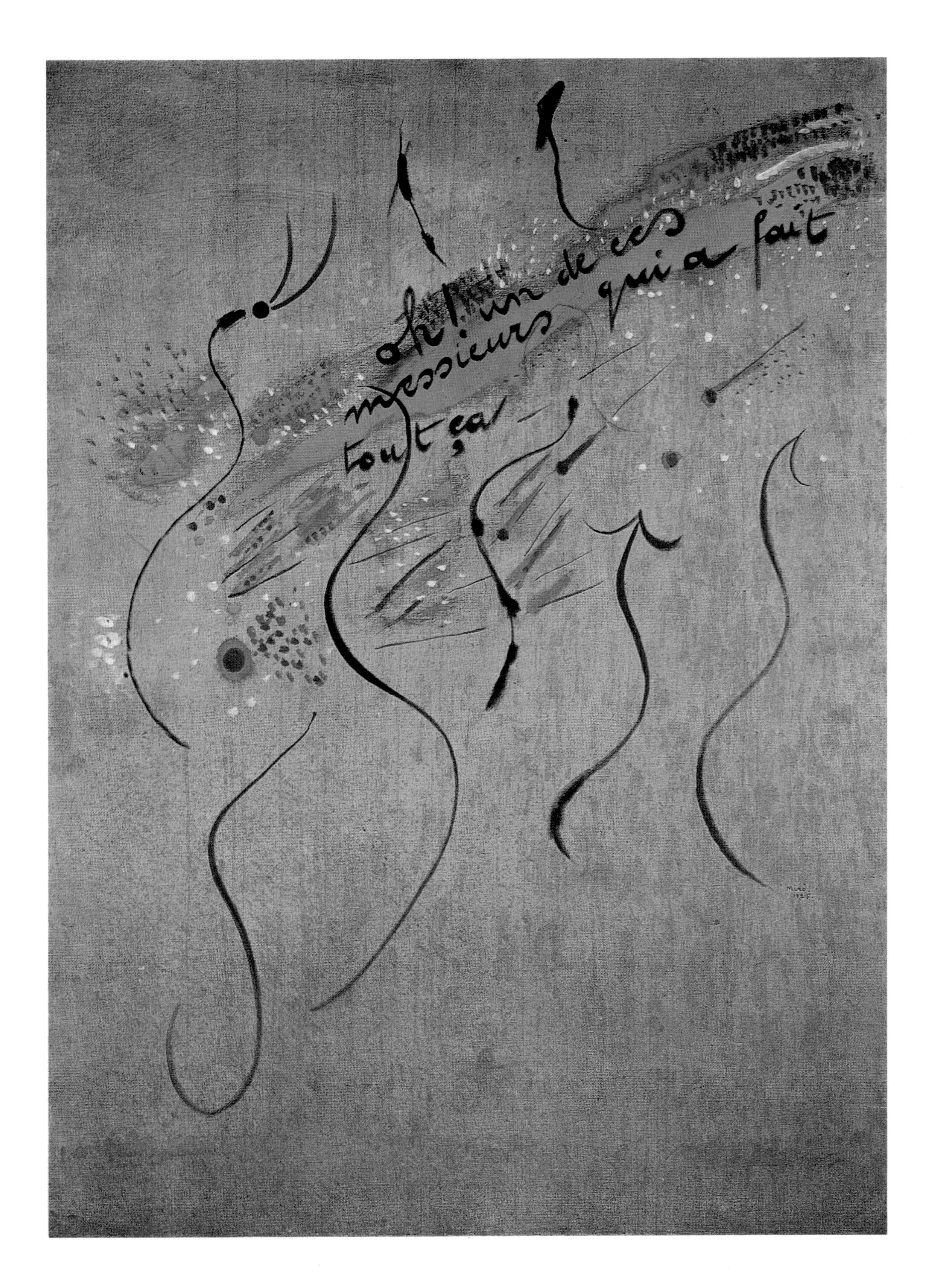
oh! un de ces
messieurs qui a fait
tout ça

Colorplate 13

YVES TANGUY (1900–1955)

Genesis

Painted in 1926
Oil on canvas, 39 1/4 × 32"
Private collection, Paris

Yves Tanguy was born in Paris and spent part of his childhood in the Finistère province of Brittany. He seems to have been impressed by that region's dolmens and menhirs. Following in the family tradition (his father had been a sea captain), he went to sea. In 1920 he was drafted into the French army, and while in the service he met Jacques Prévert; together they discovered Lautréamont's *Les Chants de Maldoror,* which the Surrealists held in high esteem, and the magazine *La Révolution surréaliste.* In 1923 Tanguy happened to see a De Chirico painting in the window of an art gallery in Paris. It had such a powerful effect on him that he decided to become a painter.

Tanguy destroyed most of his early paintings. The few remaining ones show a naive approach, a kind of Sunday painting. In 1925–26, having made contact with the Surrealists, Tanguy made a completely new start. He produced a wealth of hasty automatic sketches in which abstract and representational objects are mixed. These, along with André Masson's handwriting drawings, Miró's sketches, and occasional experiments by Max Ernst, make up the automatic phase of Surrealism about 1926.

Tanguy's early Surrealist paintings are derived from these spontaneous notations. Against a monochromatic background which seems a flat backdrop rather than a landscape, he placed the logograms he had developed in his drawings which, in *Genesis,* may stand for civilization (tower), landscape (hill), plant life (branch), and the animal world (snake). Solitary human figures and parts of human beings float freely in this diffuse picture world which also contains some geometric and stereometric objects (borrowed from the paintings of De Chirico) and letters. The combination of disparate elements may derive from proto-Surrealist paintings and collages; in any case, they create an unreal atmospheric unity which is, and is meant to be, totally subjective and hermetic. Among its sources are early paintings by Max Ernst—the tightrope walker in *Genesis* brings to mind Ernst's *The Teetering Woman* of 1923—as well as the "exquisite corpses," with their combination of clearly identifiable objects and strange, inexplicable shapes. Tanguy's early Surrealist paintings reveal—as can be seen in *Genesis*—some undigested influences. But the Surrealists' interest in his work was growing. In 1927 the Galerie Surréaliste in Paris showed pictures by Tanguy in combination with American primitive art. The preface to the catalogue was written by André Breton. In the Surrealist group shows of the following period, Tanguy was almost always included.

Colorplate 14

YVES TANGUY

The Ribbon of Extremes

Painted in 1932

Oil on wood, 13 1/2 × 7 1/2"

Private collection, London

The Ribbon of Extremes, which was reproduced in the magazine *La Révolution surréaliste* the year it was painted, marks Tanguy's transition from a diffuse atmospheric picture world to the illusionist Verism of the Improbable that was to be the trademark of his work until his death in 1955.

The purple background merges into a gray plane near the bottom of the picture. Spatial organization remains undefined—in contrast to Tanguy's later paintings. The horizon can only be guessed at behind a bank of fog. The picture does not represent a landscape. It is instead "a picture which is a landscape" (the title of another Tanguy painting, dated 1927). The reality of representation is replaced by the reality of the picture.

In the foreground and in the fogbound area, a number of three-dimensional shapes and constructions are lined up more or less parallel to the picture surface. These biomorphic shapes resemble abstract sculptures made of various unidentifiable materials. An affinity with Dali is obvious—for instance in the crutchlike props in the right half of the picture. These structures stand in definite spatial relation to each other: they cast shadows, and they appear so clearly defined as possible objects that one is amazed at not being able to identify them.

The arsenal of unreal objects is still extremely large in *The Ribbon of Extremes.* They seem to have been lined up here for the first time as a kind of survey of possible shapes. In his later work, Tanguy was to dip into this arsenal again and again, in order to obtain a constantly changing (and solidifying) pictorial scene consisting of these elements: background/floor, object/sculpture, and light/shade. His method remained the same: at first a sketch was outlined on canvas—very casually, almost automatically; then the picture was developed and executed with the utmost finesse and precision.

Colorplate 15

YVES TANGUY

The Sun in Its Shrine

Painted in 1937
Oil on canvas, 45 1/4 × 34 3/4″
Collection Peggy Guggenheim, Venice

While automatic writing, the informal-psychic component of Surrealism, was in its heyday in 1925 and 1926, the tradition of illusionist painting based on De Chirico and the early works of Max Ernst continued, playing a minor role until the emergence of Tanguy, Dali, Magritte, and Pierre Roy. Between 1924 and 1929, the periodical *La Révolution surréaliste* continued to publish reproductions of veristic, proto-Surrealist works. Once, using an example by Pierre Roy, a critic dubbed the proto-Surrealist style "Magic Realism."

The work of Tanguy, after he abandoned automatic writing in the thirties, shows traits of realism, if we consider only the manner of execution as the criterion. What is Surrealist in these works is their content, in which the unreal is made real.

From about 1932 on, Tanguy's pictures are generally simpler and more clearly organized than, say, his *Ribbon of Extremes* (colorplate 14). Where the horizon is not clearly shown—as in *The Sun in Its Shrine*—it can be guessed at from the transition of color between ground and sky, though there is no precise definition. The vagueness of spatial organization becomes even more mystifying when the artificial objects (generally fewer in number than in *The Ribbon of Extremes*) extend into the sky, where they seem not so much to float as to lie. This creates a new ambivalence: the picture presents itself as an illusionist landscape and, at the same time, as a painting that can deal arbitrarily with its subject matter—by ignoring, for instance, the generally acknowledged assumption that there is a boundary between earth and sky (the horizon) above which things cannot lie but must float.

These very precisely painted pictures give the impression that Tanguy is showing what is possible in art by creating a seeming identity between the image and that which it depicts—an identity which the viewer is bound to experience as ambiguity because what is depicted is never identical with anything his experience can recognize as a color-bearing object.

The entire series of pictures which Tanguy painted between 1937 and his death in 1955 encompasses a complete subjective world made up of artifacts and experiences—feelings of infinity, loneliness, uncertainty, and emptiness.

Colorplate 16

ANDRE MASSON (b. 1896)

Battle of Fish

Painted in 1927

Oil, sand, and pen and ink on canvas, 14 1/2 × 28 1/2"

The Museum of Modern Art, New York City

André Masson was born in Balagny (Oise), Belgium, in 1896. He studied at the Académie Royale des Beaux-Arts in Brussels and the Ecole des Beaux-Arts in Paris. In 1914 he was drafted into the army and was severely wounded in World War I. From 1922 on, he lived in Paris, where his friendship with Miró began that year. In 1924, the year of the first Surrealist manifesto, he met Aragon, Breton, and Eluard; he was a member of the Surrealist movement from the beginning and took part in all its major exhibits and activities. In 1929 he was among those whom Breton savagely attacked in his second manifesto.

Masson had been introduced to Cubism at the end of World War I. His paintings until the middle of the twenties had a definite orientation toward Analytical Cubism. When he and Breton became friends, Breton's ideas about art fell on fertile ground with Masson, especially as Masson had already been brought near that "systematic confusion of the senses" postulated by Rimbaud, through the use of alcohol and narcotics. Thus preconditioned to working from his unconscious and stimulated by the writings of Rimbaud, Lautréamont, De Sade, and the German Romantics, Masson readily followed Breton's suggestion that he take up automatism. His need for self-expression drove him beyond Cubist painting, and painting generally.

For three years, he worked in trancelike states, creating automatic drawings out of which he developed fish and bird heads. He made innumerable drawings and notations, each representing a segment of an extensive search for form and expression. His works did not try to communicate a message to the world but to discover and elucidate the artist's own self. Hence their impulsive character, reminiscent of handwriting: hence the fact that no subsequent corrections were made: the result was the drawing as psychogram.

Beginning in 1927, Masson did "sand pictures," of which *Battle of Fish* is one. He tried to translate the freedom of automatic writing into the realm of painting by spreading glue unevenly across a canvas and then pouring sand over it. The sand adhered to random sections of the canvas, creating patterns over which the artist had no control. These patterns were then modified and elaborated upon with pen and brush. In the 1927 picture, *Painting (Figure)*, paint has been squeezed directly from the tube onto the canvas. (The title is deliberately misleading, since it indicates a technique that has not been used.) In *Battle of Fish*, the technique of the casual pen and ink drawing has been transferred to the canvas. Similar to Max Ernst's *frottages*, this picture is the unpremeditated result of the interplay between accident and intention.

In the sand pictures, Masson tried to break free from the restrictions and rules of painting. What has been gained is a kind of breakthrough, an art that transcends the boundaries of the conventional picture. The thematic content of *Battle of Fish* and similar works is the trauma of war translated into the animal world. In 1917 Max Ernst had produced a similar transformation with a watercolor called the *Battle of Fish*. War and death are important themes in Masson's work; during that period he expressed these themes through his dominant motifs, the bird and the fish.

In evolving figures and objects from random patterns, Masson works in a manner similar to Miró's (blobs of sand and red paint take on the meaning of hills, of blood, in the context of the picture). This method is the opposite of abstraction: it serves the creation of objective pictures based on the products of the unconscious. In a conversation with Matisse in 1932, Masson is said to have remarked: "I begin without an image or plan in mind, but just draw or paint rapidly according to my impulses. Gradually, in the marks I make, I see suggestions of figures or objects. I encourage these to emerge, trying to bring out their implications even as I now consciously try to give order to the composition." To which Matisse supposedly replied: "That's curious. With me it's just the reverse. I always start with something—a chair, a table—but as the work proceeds, I become less conscious of it. By the end, I am hardly aware of the subject with which I started" (bibl. 43).

Colorplate 17

ANDRE MASSON

Gradiva

Painted in 1939

Oil on canvas, 38 × 51″

Collection Nellens, Knokke, Belgium

In 1934 Masson settled in Tossa, Catalonia. In 1936 he was driven away by the Spanish Civil War, and he went to Paris. The war in Spain engaged his imagination. In a series of horrifying paintings, he showed his sympathy for the sufferings of the oppressed. He castigated the fascist coalition of state, army, and church in satirical drawings (fig. 74). In 1941 Masson left Paris and fled to the United States, where he lived for four years in the New York City area.

Masson's first Surrealist phase (1924–29) was followed by a series of Massacres (1930–34) and other pictures that are statements about the Spanish Civil War. A second Surrealist phase began in 1937 and lasted until 1941. Expressive deformation dominates his work of that period.

One of Dali's paintings of the thirties is called *Gradiva Rediscovers the Ruins of the Anthropomorphous* and Dali calls his wife, Gala, Gradiva—"she who advances." Gradiva was the name of Breton's Surrealist gallery in the rue de Seine in Paris, before World War II, and *Gradiva* is the title of the picture shown here. Who is Gradiva?

Gradiva is the leading character in a story by the German writer Wilhelm Jensen (1837–1911) which Sigmund Freud has analyzed in his essay "Delusions and Dreams in W. Jensen's *Gradiva*" (1907). Freud's essay must have made a profound impression on the Surrealists. Werner Spies (bibl. 98) has proved conclusively that the remarkable painting *Au Premier mot limpide* by Max Ernst is based on a Gradiva motif. The picture is one of a recently rediscovered series of decorations Max Ernst created for Paul Eluard's house in Eubonne (1923).

In Jensen's story, an archaeologist, Norbert Hanold, buys a plaster cast of a statue he has seen in Rome that fascinates him. It is the statue of a young woman (Gradiva) in mid-stride. One night, Hanold has "a terrifying dream": "He found himself in ancient Pompeii on August 24, in the year 79, the very day on which the dreadful eruption of Vesuvius occurred. . . . The masses of flame, billowing from the crater, allowed only occasional glimpses of things, suffused by blood-red light." Hanold remains unscathed. "While standing at the edge of the forum, near the Temple of Jupiter, he suddenly saw Gradiva, only a short distance away. . . . He recognized her at first glance; her stone image had been accurate in every detail, including the manner of her stride." Hanold wants to warn her, but she walks on. "But her face became ever paler, as if she were being transformed into white marble. She advanced as far as the portico of the temple, but there she seated herself on a step between two columns and slowly lowered her head until it touched the stone. . . . She lay there . . . on the wide step, as if asleep, but she had stopped breathing, she had apparently suffocated from the sulfur vapors. The red glare from Vesuvius flickered across her face which, with its closed eyes, looked exactly like her beautiful stone image."

It is this dream which Masson has painted—the position of the feet is exactly as described in Jensen's book. In the story, the dream partly comes true: Hanold encounters a young woman in modern Pompeii. In his mind, he calls her Gradiva because she resembles the statue, and because he sees her sitting in the position of the dream, like "one of the young girls who had found death among these ashes."

What interested Freud and the Surrealists in this rather trivial story must have been the interaction of dream, reality, and history on the one hand, and the symbolism of certain events in the story on the other. Gradiva is, as statue, made of stone; is a dream image that turns to stone; is a living figure. Freud interprets Hanold's Gradiva psychoanalytically. He sees archaeological experiences as analogies to psychoanalysis: the experience of being buried is an image of repression, the act of excavation an image of psychoanalysis.

What is Surrealist about Masson's picture is not so much the method by which it is produced as its relationship to Freud: the interest in Jensen's way of placing reality and consciousness on the same plane. Like Freud, Masson contributes toward making the invisible visible, by indicating the sexual connotations at which Jensen merely hints with such visual elements as the wide open, shell-like vagina of the figure.

Colorplate 18

PIERRE ROY (1880–1950)

Rural Electrification

Painted in 1930

Oil on canvas, 28 1/4 × 20 3/4"

Wadsworth Atheneum, Hartford, Connecticut. Sumner Collection

Though Pierre Roy was represented in the first Surrealist show in 1925 at the Galerie Pierre in Paris and in every important subsequent group show (his *Rural Electrification* was shown at The Museum of Modern Art in New York in 1936 in the exhibition *Fantastic Art, Dada and Surrealism*), he has remained largely unknown. His paintings, dating from about 1930, belong with the illusionist-verist branch of Surrealism—with Dali, Magritte, and Tanguy.

Pierre Roy was born in Nantes in 1880. He studied in Paris, where he made contact with the Fauves. About 1925, De Chirico arranged for him to meet Aragon, Breton, Eluard, and Max Ernst.

In 1927 or 1928, he painted *Danger on the Stairs,* in which the view of a perfectly ordinary solid stairway in a middle-class interior is marred by the appearance of a snake. This demonization of a precisely portrayed environment is based on the Surrealist practice of combining incompatible elements, of depicting the improbable. The practice produces shock because it runs counter to everyday experience. Such constellations, first created by Max Ernst in his picture novels, were later reintroduced by artists like Dorothea Tanning.

In Pierre Roy's work such shock effects are rare. He depicts reality with painstaking precision, and in that respect he could be called a realist. The difference lies in *what* he depicts. *Rural Electrification* is a view of a flat landscape with a very low horizon and thus a very low viewing angle. In the distance we see a row of electric poles which runs diagonally away from the viewer. A round wooden platform lies in the foreground, to which are attached four upright bamboo poles. These carry variously shaped pieces of paper. There are also two half-full glasses on the platform, and a bamboo pole, horizontally resting on top of the glasses, has a spotted egg hanging from it by a red string.

"Most of my work is done from childhood memories. Unconsciously I incorporated the kind of toys in my pictures that I used to make for myself out of bamboo poles, empty cartridge shells, seashells, nuts, grain, paper straws, girls' hair ribbons, and candy boxes" (Roy, bibl. 132).

What is unusual in Roy's perspective ("De Chirico has most certainly influenced me," Roy has said) is this: the "toys" are huge, while the landscape with the electric stanchions which give the picture its title is tiny. This could be simply the result of the mole's-eye view, except that in this picture the deliberately created disproportions (after all, the angle of perspective had not been given, it had to be chosen) express the Surrealist stance of protest against civilization: small personal objects hold their own against electrification —which represents the industrialization of the environment.

Roy's pictures are by no means realistic, even though they employ realistic elements of style. The way in which landscape and a repertoire of personal objects are combined, and the way they are put in perspective, is too contradictory and too strange to be called realistic.

Colorplate 19

SALVADOR DALI (b. 1904)

Illumined Pleasures

Painted in 1929

Oil and collage on wood, 9 1/4 × 13 1/2"

The Museum of Modern Art, New York City. Harriet and Sidney Janis Collection

Dali was born in 1904 in Figueras, Catalonia, where he took drawing lessons during World War I. In 1921 he went to Madrid to study; there he met Federico García Lorca and Luis Buñuel. Until 1926–27—when he was expelled from the Academia de San Fernando and took his first trip to Paris—his paintings were influenced in turn by the style of Vermeer, De Chirico, the Cubists, and Picasso's classicist period. Between 1928 and 1929 he did his first Surrealist paintings, under the influence of Ernst and Tanguy. Miró introduced Dali to the Parisian circle of Surrealists. In 1929 he had his first one-man show at the Galerie Goemans in Paris (catalogue preface by André Breton). During the previous year he had collaborated with Buñuel on the film *Un Chien Andalou.*

At a time of repeated crises and a growing number of expulsions from the Surrealist group, Dali's participation provided a fresh impetus. His eccentricity breathed fresh life into the movement. His influence was enormous. His showmanship and his painting enlarged the possibilities of Surrealism.

Later Dali was to say that he had merely wanted to use the Surrealist group as a springboard: "Although I plunged into the craziest ventures with the same eagerness as they, I was already laying—with Macchiavellian skepticism—the structural foundation for the next step in the eternal tradition. The Surrealists seemed the only ones who formed a group whose methods would serve my plans. Their leader, André Breton, seemed irreplaceable in his function as visible head of the movement. As for me, I tried to lead, but by means of a secret influence, both opportunistic and contradictory" (*The Secret Life of Salvador Dali,* New York, 1942). In 1968 he asserted: "The difference between the Surrealists and me is the fact that I am a Surrealist" (*Les Passions selon Dali,* Zurich and Paris, 1968).

One of the most concentrated pictures of the first Surrealist phase in Dali's work is *Illumined Pleasures.* Three boxes whose front panels look like framed pictures are standing on a plain beneath a blue sky. They are surrounded by an assortment of figures. The manner of painting is extremely precise: the photocollage showing the side of a church in the box on the left has exactly the same quality of realism—apart from its monochromatic color scheme—as the painted sections. And yet, the picture is marked by the collage principle: a wealth of disparate motifs are combined on the picture surface, and it is impossible to discover a unifying theme at first glance.

William S. Rubin, in his book on Surrealism (bibl. 43), has produced a first analysis of this picture which is extremely convincing. Rubin maintains that these enigmatic early works by Dali are more easily explained, can in fact be explained only through the recurrence of symbols in different contexts and the adoption of elements taken from De Chirico and Max Ernst.

In this phase, Dali's preoccupation is mainly with himself. Stimulated by Freud's writings, he expresses childhood experiences in borrowed or original metaphors. In the central picture box, there is an insect that may be a locust or grasshopper, or a praying mantis, above a horizontal self-portrait. As a child, Dali experienced a fear of grasshoppers and in fact called himself a "grasshopper child." He also had a fear of being devoured: the praying mantis devours its male partner after the sex act. Anxiety and menace in the man-woman relationship are implied in the snarling lion and the woman's head (which is also a pitcher—vessels are symbols for women in Freudian psychology), and in the foreground scene: a bearded man (borrowed from De Chirico and Max Ernst—see figs. 14 and 15) holds a female figure whose hands are bloody; to the left of this scene a severed hand is holding a bloody knife and is held, in turn, by another hand. The idea of being devoured during the sex act suggests that there is safety in masturbation—and this is symbolized by the rear-view figure of a young man leaning against the right side of the central box (there is a still more obvious reference in *Loneliness,* 1931). Dali himself has called the biomorphic shapes we see on the heads of the bicycle riders in the box at the right "the sugar almonds of the Playa Confitera that provoke masturbation." The young man hiding his face also symbolizes castration fear—Rubin points out that Dali's interpretation of the William Tell story shows this as well. And, of course, the bloody knife can also be interpreted in this context. Several of these motifs frequently recur in Dali's work; their repetition in various guises makes Rubin's kind of interpretation convincing in the case of certain pictures.

If, on the one hand, we see Max Ernst's influence on Dali—in the father-son group and the bird motifs (along a totem pole to the left of the center box)—De Chirico, on the other hand, seems to play an even larger part in this picture. The mannequin head broken open to reveal a hair-swirl or toupée, the motif of the prodigal son (in the background), the pictures within the picture, and the distorted shadows all stem from De Chirico's iconographic repertoire. (In the right foreground there is a direct quotation from De Chirico: the shadow of a figure that does not appear in the picture.) These borrowed and original elements are all combined into a collage painting with a complicated message. The theme is Dali's recognition of his own sexual and psychological problems.

Colorplate 20

SALVADOR DALI

The Persistence of Memory

Painted in 1931
Oil on canvas, 9 1/2 × 13"
The Museum of Modern Art, New York City

About 1930, Dali developed his theory of a "paranoiac-critical method." Paranoia is expressed in chronic delusions, hallucinations, delusions of grandeur, persecution mania, and castration fear. Dali does not regard himself as a paranoiac; rather, he wishes to produce paranoiac conditions by an act of will: "The only difference between me and a madman is that I am not mad." Two samples of Dali's contradictory definitions of his paranoiac-critical method are: "a spontaneous assimilation of irrational knowledge based on the critical and systematic objectification of delirious phenomena," or "a spontaneous method of irrational knowledge through interpretative-critical associations of phenomena of insanity." Most of these ideas appear in Dali's essay, *La Femme visible,* published in 1930 in Paris.

In the visual realm, the paranoiac-critical method manifests itself mainly in the ability (which can, but needn't, be called hallucinatory) to see different objects "into" certain things. Whereas Max Ernst developed objects out of random shapes, Dali strives for visual identity between two disparate objects. See, for instance, the double image of woman's head and pitcher in his *Illumined Pleasures* (colorplate 19).

While Dali based his early pictures on extremely personal childhood memories and dreams, the 1930s saw him turning more and more toward a repertory of general symbols derived from psychiatric and psychoanalytical literature. He was obsessed "with castration, putrefaction, voyeurism, onanism, coprophilia, and impotence . . ." (Rubin, bibl. 43). James Thrall Soby has pointed out that "Dali's Surrealist pictures are practically crawling with fetishes straight out of Krafft-Ebing's case histories—house slippers, keys, hair, and so on" (bibl. 74). Thus, Dali's pictures are not to be interpreted psychoanalytically. Rather, they exploit the discoveries of psychoanalysis. Freud corroborates this in his commentary on Dali when he says that the things that came to Leonardo unconsciously were consciously utilized by Dali.

Fear of impotence plays an important part. In *The Persistence of Memory,* another small-size painting, we see an amorphous shape lying in a landscape whose horizon reaches three-quarters up toward the top of the picture. On the left is a platform with a dead tree that has grown out of it. Clock faces are draped over the platform, over a limb of the tree, and across the amorphous shape which actually is a mouthless self-portrait. If we accept the mouth as a symbol for the female sex organ, the absence of a mouth can be interpreted as a projection of impotence anxiety onto the sexual partner. The mouth, incidentally, appears in various guises in Surrealist painting. In the Dali-Buñuel film *Un Chien Andalou,* a mouth vanishes and is replaced by ancillary hair. In Dali's paintings *The Great Masturbator* (1929) and *The Lugubrious Game* (1932), an insect like a praying mantis is seen sitting on a mouth; in *The Dream* (1932), there are ants in place of a mouth. Magritte, in *The Rape* (1934), supplants a mouth with pubic hair (and puts breasts in the place of eyes, a navel in the place of a nose).

According to Marcel Jean (in bibl. 38), the soft clocks, too, symbolize impotence. For Marcel Jean, *montre* does not only mean "clock" but also the imperative form of the verb *montrer* (to show). The sick child must show his tongue to the doctor *(montrer la molle)* which sounds the same as "soft clock" *(la montre molle).* "The clocks in *The Persistence of Memory* look more like tongues than anything else." In *Uranium and Atomica Melancholica Idyll,* a clock is transformed into a tongue. Also, tongue-like shapes are often seen propped on crutches in Dali's work. Thus the clock, like the tongue and those tongue-like shapes, may be a "symbol for a limp penis." The combination of soft clock and soft version of the key symbol in *Soft Clocks—Soft Alarm Clock* (1933) seems to support this somewhat bold interpretation.

Dali's own commentary on the soft-clock motif rather obscures the issue: "Rest assured, the famous soft clocks are merely the soft, crazy, lonely, paranoid-critical Camembert of time and space" (Dali, *Conquest of the Irrational,* New York, 1935). A manuscript by Dali, containing his interpretation of *The Persistence of Memory,* has thus far remained unpublished.

Colorplate 21

SALVADOR DALI

Portrait of Gala

Painted in 1935

Oil on wood, 12 3/4 × 10 1/2"

The Museum of Modern Art, New York City. Gift of Mrs. John D. Rockefeller, Jr.

In *Portrait of Gala,* a rear and a frontal view of the same female figure (Gala) are seen facing each other like mirror images. There is a picture on the wall, a variation on *The Angelus* (1859) by Jean-François Millet. The *Portrait of Gala* is less enigmatic than most of Dali's work. The title explains the picture. The subtitle, *The Angelus of Gala,* stresses the interrelation between Millet's and Dali's motifs, as shown in the picture: the frontally seen Gala is seated on a wheelbarrow, just like the female figure in Dali's version of the Millet painting.

Dali himself reports that there had been a reproduction of Millet's picture on the wall of his classroom when he was a child and that it had made a strong impression on him. "The picture produced a vague but powerful fear in me, so that the memory of those two motionless silhouettes stayed with me for many years." This fascination was not caused by the picture's sentimental content but by a discovery which Dali expressed pictorially in one of the etchings he made for a 1934 edition of Lautréamont's *Les Chants de Maldoror:* the peasant is hiding his erect penis with his cap. To Dali's eye the woman is pregnant, and the pitchfork is stuck in the earth (which symbolizes the female principle). In Dali's 1934 etching, the pitchfork is driven into the woman's pelvis. There is a pen-and-ink sketch after this etching in which the woman threatens the man's erect penis with a large knife, reminiscent of the woman with the bloody hands and of the bloody knife in *Illumined Pleasures* (see Rubin, bibl. 43). Dali's paranoiac-critical method makes him see sexual repression in Millet's devotional painting. Freud's analysis of Leonardo's *The Virgin and Child with Saint Anne* may have played a part in this: Freud sees indications of a homosexual neurosis in Leonardo's painting.

About 1933, Dali did several variations on Millet's *Angelus: Atavism of Twilight, Meditation on the Harp,* and *Gala and the Angelus of Millet Immediately Preceding the Arrival of the Conic Anamorphosis.* In the latter, Gala, Maxim Gorky, and Lenin are shown posed under a reproduction of Millet's picture.

By repeating the wheelbarrow in his *Portrait of Gala,* Dali moves it from the reality level of the picture within the picture into the reality level of the portrait. At the same time, he leaves the gender of the massive rear-view figure open to conjecture, so that the constellation in Millet's picture seems to repeat itself in the portrait. Thus, the two-dimensional picture within the picture would be changed into a three-dimensional picture scene, viewed from a different angle (tautological effects are very frequent with Dali, as can be seen from the notes on his other works in this book).

Furthermore, the large rear-view figure suggests the idea that it is taking the place of the viewer. Thus Dali draws the reality of the viewer into the reality level of the portrait. These three levels—the reality of the artist or viewer, of the portrait, and of the picture within the picture—must be kept separate, for it seems that this is Dali's pictorial comment on the production of art in general: his work (the portrait) is the result of an encounter between himself (reality) and that original impetus that is now being quoted as a picture within the picture.

As he so often did in the thirties, Dali has here used the means of an almost photographic realism. The formât and technique are deliberately in the style of the old masters. The texture of the jackets with their design of raised embroidery reminds one of Vermeer, whom Dali has quoted on occasion (see *Appearance of the City of Delft,* 1935–36).

Colorplate 22

SALVADOR DALI

Soft Construction with Boiled Beans: A Premonition of Civil War

Painted in 1936

Oil on canvas, 39 1/2 × 33"

Museum of Art, Philadelphia. Louise and Walter Arensberg Collection

The Surrealists, who were more or less antifascist, and Dali were bound to come to a parting of the ways when the political development in Germany mobilized all of the Surrealists' defenses while Dali proclaimed his liking for Hitler. Twenty years later, he was to write: "I was fascinated by Hitler's soft, fleshy back which was always strapped so tightly into his uniform. Every time I began to paint the leather strap that ran from his belt across one shoulder, the softness of this Hitler-flesh, compressed by the tunic, put me into a shameful, nourishing, Wagnerian ecstasy which made my heart beat violently . . ." ("Dali Says . . .," Munich, 1968).

In 1934 Dali was banished from the Surrealist group. The speech he made in his own defense at Breton's studio is said to have been one of his best performances, although the political attitude it expressed ran counter to all reason. With a thermometer in his mouth, going through a sophisticated striptease, he declared that his paintings were a transmission of dreams which, according to the Surrealists' own manifesto, must under no circumstances be censured or controlled. He could not help it if his dreams were of Millet's *Angelus* and of Hitler, and he had every right to paint and appreciate these dreams.

Up until 1934, his works had been exhibited in galleries that were chiefly devoted to Surrealism: in 1931, 1932, and 1933 at the Pierre Colle Gallery in Paris; in 1933 and 1934 at the Julien Levy Gallery in New York. He took part in most of the Surrealist group shows.

In 1936 the Spanish Civil War began. While such artists as Picasso, Masson, and Miró declared for the Republicans, Dali—while fairly reticent in his utterances—was unmistakably on the side of Franco. "Before Franco there was no politician and no new government that didn't add to the confusion, disorder, and lies rampant in Spain. Franco has violently broken with this false tradition, he has restored clarity, truth, and order to the country" (Dali, 1951). To his grotesque style, which combines the technique of the old masters with extroverted obsessions, he added grotesque political opinions. His "main hope for the future" was "a religious renaissance," but also "an anarchistic absolute king." He stated that "Ludwig II of Bavaria was not such a bad king after all!"

No doubt, Dali's countless comments on everything and anything are not always to be taken verbatim. Like his exhibitions, they are designed to spread terror and bear witness to his genius via self-mystification. Always provocative, they nevertheless are lacking in that anti-authoritarian, inspirative quality that characterizes Surrealist art.

His contradictory personality shows him glorifying dictatorial power on the one hand while, on the other, he paints a picture like *Soft Construction with Boiled Beans,* one of his most impressive and terrifying works. The collage-like multiplicity of motifs in his *Illumined Pleasures* (colorplate 19) has now been replaced by a single powerful figure. Even without the subtitle, *Premonition of Civil War,* the picture would be interpreted as an indictment of atrocious power; one is reminded of *Saturn Devouring One of His Children* (painted between 1814 and 1819), one of Goya's series of so-called Black Paintings.

"The upper, female part is surmounted by a head whose face mirrors utter horror, boundless despair, and inhuman pain. The grotesque dimensions which call to mind the most abnormal pathological distortions, like arms growing out of a hip, one hand gripping a red inflamed breast, a leg coming out of a shoulder—these are not merely a monstrous vision of the Spanish Civil War but of war . . . as such" (bibl. 29).

Colorplate 23

SALVADOR DALI

Cannibalism in Autumn

Painted in 1936–37
Oil on canvas, 31 1/2 × 31 1/2"
The Tate Gallery, London. Loaned by Edward James

The theme of *Soft Construction with Boiled Beans* is given another variation in this picture. Dali himself has pointed to the connection with the Spanish Civil War: "Those Iberian creatures devouring each other in the fall express the pathos of civil war, interpreted (by me) as a phenomenon of natural history, in contrast to Picasso who interprets it as a political phenomenon." Apart from the fact that war is certainly not at all a natural phenomenon, this picture demonstrates the self-dismemberment of a people. At the same time, the artist refuses to show any party preference whatsoever, disregards political issues, and indulges in a certain amount of aestheticism.

In an extremely serene landscape, two figures on a table flow into each other (that is, belong together). They are attacking each other with knife and fork and other eating utensils. The remnants of food on the table indicate that a meal, a kind of peaceful companionship, has been broken off so that the parties can maim each other.

In spite of its surprise elements—meat and apple on the man's head, ants in the woman's face, and her immensely long, outflowing breast—the picture is much more concentrated than much of Dali's work, especially the late paintings. Again, there is the Surrealist principle of conscious combinations of incompatible elements: the beautiful landscape and charming still life confronted by the cruel scene; the human figures transformed into some smooth material that gives them the look of sculpture; the seriousness of bodily injury contradicted by this harmonious, soft material. The general attitude toward the war is crisscrossed here by personal symbols (ants, apple, bread, crutch, sugar almonds, drawer): the subjective associations obscure the clearly presented scenery. And this provocative material is handled with the technique of the old masters (Dali aspired to the accomplishments of Vermeer and Meissonier).

Undoubtedly this picture must be considered Surrealist. Yet it is difficult to imagine a greater contrast between two artists than, say, Max Ernst (whose *Breakfast in the Grass* of 1935–36 has some aspects in common with *Cannibalism in Autumn*) and Dali, though both belonged to the Surrealist movement. Dali stands for quiet and order, Ernst for restlessness and doubt. Dali embraces a Catholic mysticism while Ernst espouses an enlightened anticlericalism. Dali wants to be a genius; Ernst attacks the irrationalism of the genius cult. Dali paints like an old master; Ernst replaces painterly techniques with other, inspirative ones. Ernst represents a consciousness that criticizes the conventions and takes issue with a world devastated by war and the preparation for war. He takes issue with inhumanity, with bourgeois attitudes, sexual repression, and the heritage of intolerance handed down by the Victorian parent generation. Dali glorifies himself in self-representations; he mystifies rather than enlightens ("I *am* the drug"). With his perfect, unreal pictures, Dali stupefies, whereas Ernst stimulates with his open ones.

But, like Max Ernst, Salvador Dali is a many-faceted artist. In 1927 he produced his first stage setting—for Lorca's *Mariana Pineda* in Barcelona—which was followed by numerous others, for Léonide Massine (New York, 1939, 1941, and 1944), Luchino Visconti (*As You Like It,* Rome, 1948), Peter Brook (*Salome,* London, 1949), Maurice Bejart (Venice, 1961), and others. He has illustrated and written a large number of books, has collaborated with Buñuel on his early films, designed bizarre jewelry and the Lip Sofa of Mae West (1936–37), and has created objects and sculpture (*Venus de Milo of the Drawers,* 1936; see fig. 44). His countless inventions—though many of them exist only on paper—are based on the same principle of incongruous combination as many of his later paintings.

Colorplate 24

SALVADOR DALI

The Temptation of Saint Anthony

Painted in 1946

Oil on canvas, 35 1/4 × 47"

Musées Royaux des Beaux-Arts de Belgique, Brussels

Having spent the 1930s in Rome, New York, and London, but considering himself on the whole a Parisian, Dali was forced to flee the German occupation of France in 1940. He went to Spain and then to the United States for several years. His first great retrospective was mounted by The Museum of Modern Art in New York (1941–42) from where it traveled to eight other American cities. Dali's fame was firmly established by then, especially in the United States.

In 1945–46, Dali took part in a competition organized by the American motion-picture producer Albert Levin in conjunction with a film based on *Bel-Ami* by De Maupassant. Levin needed a painting for it, showing the temptation of Saint Anthony. Eleven painters took part in the competition, among them Leonora Carrington, Dali, Paul Delvaux, Max Ernst, and Dorothea Tanning. The jurors were Alfred H. Barr, Jr., Marcel Duchamp, and Sidney Janis, who had published the essay *Abstract and Surrealist Art in America* the previous year (1944). The prize went to Max Ernst. His *Temptation of Saint Anthony* is based on the Temptation in the Isenheim altarpiece (c. 1510–15) by Grünewald.

Dali's version of this traditional subject also reaches back into art history, but it does so by playing with profundities that emphasize symbolic meanings. Saint Anthony is seen kneeling in the left foreground on a low-lying plain, across which a caravan of spider-legged animals approaches: a rearing horse with horseshoes twisted sideways and four elephants bearing various burdens on their backs (a naked woman, an obelisk, architectural fragments, and a column). Parts of the Escorial appear carried in a cloud.

In Max Ernst's picture, the temptations are depicted—as they are in Grünewald's—as hideous, androgynous monsters. Dali, on the other hand, used a set of symbols that aspire to a complex spiritual world in the medieval sense.

Saint Anthony, equipped with the traditional cross (to ward off the evil spirits) and human skull, is confronted by a number of iconographic elements. The horse represents both coercive power and aggressive sensuality. The first elephant carries the chalice of lust, from which emerges a naked woman squeezing her breasts. Even more than the elephant bearing the obelisk—a reference to Bernini's sculpture in Rome—the Baroque church facade framing a female torso (a motif previously used by Magritte, Delvaux, and Duchamp) shows the perversion of the spiritual by the worldly.

The cloud-borne vision of the Escorial must be regarded as the ideal opposite: a symbol, not of the corruption of the spiritual by the temporal, but of the union of temporal and spiritual power.

In contrast to other Surrealists who aimed at a rational, enlightened attitude toward church and state, hierarchy and mystification, Dali professed and affirmed medieval ideas in this kind of painting.

The picture is signed "Gala Salvador Dali." Elena Diakanova, born in Russia and called Gala, the "Surrealist muse," was first married to Paul Eluard and later married Dali, who acted out his idolization of her in hymnlike essays and utterances as well as by incorporating her name in his signature.

Colorplate 25

RENE MAGRITTE (1898–1967)

The Menaced Assassin

Painted in 1926

Oil on canvas, 59 × 76 3/4"

The Museum of Modern Art, New York. The Kay Sage Foundation

Rene Magritte was born in 1898 in Lessines, Belgium; he studied at the Académie des Beaux-Arts in Brussels during the last years of World War I. A reproduction of a De Chirico painting which he saw in 1922 made a deep impression on him. Together with E. L. T. Mesens, Camille Goemans, Marcel Lecomte, and Paul Nougé, he formed a kind of Belgian Surrealist group. In 1927 he moved to Le Perreux-sur-Marne near Paris, where he established close ties with Breton and Eluard. But their theoretical and personal controversy did not interest him very much, and so he moved back to Brussels in 1930 and stayed there until his death in 1967.

Magritte began as a Cubist, and painted his first Surrealist pictures after 1925. *The Menaced Assassin* is one of these. The picture tells an easily understandable story, or rather part of a story, about a crime, just as the title indicates. The situation is unequivocal, much in contrast to Magritte's later work, where pictures and their titles (added later) often have no rational connection.

We are looking into a room (the middle ground of the picture) in which an evidently dead woman lies on a couch. Her face is bloody. A man stands listening to a gramophone. His hat and coat on a chair, and a suitcase on the floor nearby, make us understand that he is merely a transient. Outside the entrance to the room (in the foreground) two men stand waiting. They are placed symmetrically and they look alike. One carries a club, the other a net. In the background we see a window with a mountain landscape beyond and three watchful faces looking into the room. If we accept the picture's invitation to guess at what has gone before and what will happen next, we reach this conclusion: a murderer is spending a moment listening to beautiful music while his captors stand ready to apprehend him. There is no escape, because the window, too, has been blocked.

To find so trivial a story worthy of art is typical for a Surrealist. The Paris Surrealists of the twenties, in their manifestos, pamphlets, and explications, discussed murders, the love life of Charlie Chaplin, the Marquis de Sade, and Nosferatu (the German Dracula). Jack the Ripper and a sex murderer named Haarman were in vogue (sex murders were favored picture subjects for Otto Dix and George Grosz, for instance). Magritte, in his early years, wrote detective stories (no longer extant), and he liked reading Poe and Stevenson, Nick Carter and Nat Pinkerton, Rex Stout, and Dashiell Hammett. He went to the movies mainly to see films by Chaplin or Fritz Lang. He liked a series of novels written between 1912 and 1914 by Pierre Souvestre and Marcel Allain called *Fantômas,* and a film serial of the same name by Louis Feuillades (1913). In 1928 Magritte published a description of the pursuit of Fantômas by an inspector of the Sûreté and, that same year, he painted *The Savage,* which contained references to a *Fantômas* book jacket. In 1953 Magritte published a grotesque, laconic description of a day in the life of Nat Pinkerton (bibl. 115).

Suzi Gablik, in her monograph on Magritte, points out the kinship that exists between Fantômas and the central figure in Lautréamont's *Les Chants de Maldoror*—a figure much revered by the Surrealists. Both are personifications of the diabolic, of evil. Fantômas is a lowbrow version of Maldoror. Both are valued by the Surrealists for their eccentricity, which flies in the face of the middle-class system. Suzi Gablik assumes that *The Menaced Assassin* is based on an episode from *Fantômas.*

This type of picture does not stand alone in Magritte's work of the mid-twenties, but at that time he also painted pictures replete with isolated fragments of objects set in landscapes reminiscent of Tanguy, and mysterious conglomerates of objects in the vein of De Chirico. In a letter dated 1965, Magritte discussed the very intense stimulus he received from the work of the Italian proto-Surrealist: "It was in fact in 1922 when I first came to know the works of Chirico. A friend then showed me a reproduction of his painting, *The Song of Love,* which I always consider to be a work by the greatest painter of our time in the sense that it deals with poetry's ascendancy over painting and the various manners of painting. Chirico was the first to dream of *what must be painted* and not *how to paint*" (bibl. 111).

Magritte has also described the impression which Max Ernst's pictures had made on him: "In illustrating *Répétitions* by Paul Eluard, Max Ernst has demonstrated magnificently that through collages obtained from old magazine illustrations, one could easily surpass everything which gives traditional painting its prestige" (bibl. 111). Magritte created a whole series of collages during the late twenties. They are mainly landscapes with segments from reproductions and printed music pasted into them.

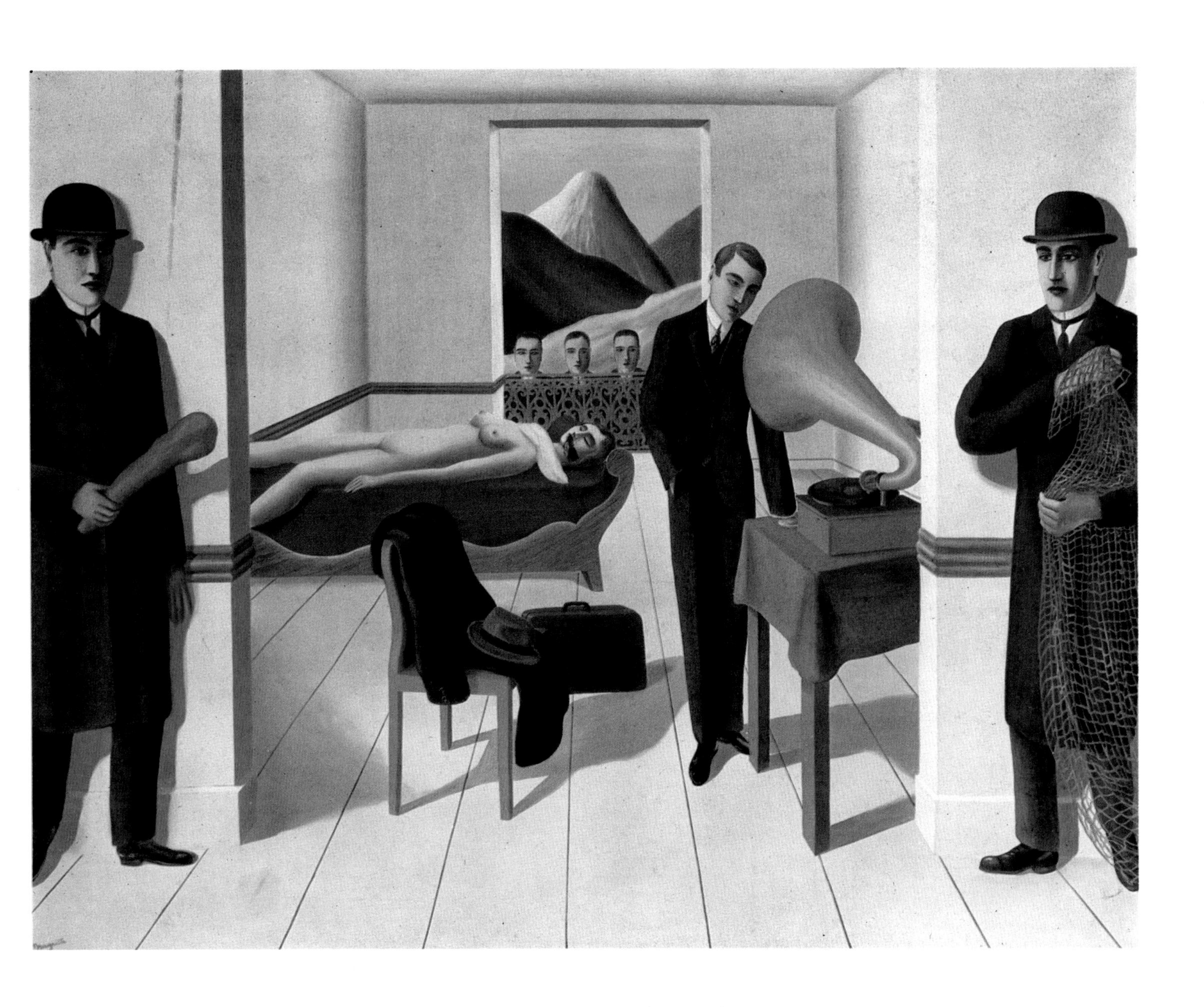

Colorplate 26

RENE MAGRITTE

On the Threshold of Liberty

Painted in 1929

Oil on canvas, 44 × 57 5/8"

Museum Boymans–van Beuningen, Rotterdam

Magritte's work is characterized by a certain number of pictorial problems. If we reduce them to a few basic themes and principles we can distinguish among 1) pictures that deal with the relationship between image and object; 2) pictures dealing with the semantic relationship between image and idea; 3) pictures which, in true Surrealist fashion, combine incongruous elements; and 4) those which, by way of metamorphosis, change people into objects or alien materials.

The Human Condition, I (colorplate 27) belongs to the first category. In the second category, we might mention *The Wind and the Song* (1928–29) and its many variations. The caption "This is not a pipe" under the picture of a pipe points to the fact that an image is merely a sign and not identical with the object it depicts. In the third category of combinatory pictures we find, for example, the nocturnal street beneath a bright sky (*Empire of Light,* 1954) and the replacement of a man's torso by a birdcage (*The Therapeutist,* 1937). Belonging to the fourth group are the transition of shoes into feet (*The Red Model,* 1935) and people, animals, and objects turned into stone, as in *The Domain of Arnheim,* 1962 (colorplate 30).

On the Threshold of Liberty fits none of these categories exactly, though there are several earlier pictures with related themes. Like Max Ernst in his Paintings for Young People, Magritte here displays several of the motifs that keep recurring in his work.

We are looking into a room in which a cannon is pointed toward the rear wall. The walls of the room consist of framed pictures. While some of these look like wallpaper, others are definitely paintings; a third group—the forest, the sky, the housefront—represent exterior views which could be either paintings or actual views from a window. The cannon is pointed at the sky-painting or the sky-view, depending on how we decide to see it. Magritte painted a variant of this picture in 1937.

The combination of different motifs in a single picture seems to have preoccupied Magritte since 1928. That year, he painted two pictures with the same title, *The Empty Mask.* One of these shows an irregularly shaped panel divided into six sections of different sizes and shapes within which the motifs of sky, parapet, and facade (upper row), and paper-cutout curtain, forest, and fire (bottom row) are disposed. The other version shows, in the four sections of a similar panel, merely the inscriptions *"ciel"* (sky), *"corps humain (ou forêt)"* (human body or forest), *"rideau"* (curtain), *"façade de maison"* (housefront). A juxtaposition of image and idea is given in *The Palace of Curtains, III* (1928–29), in which we see two frames; one contains a picture of the sky, the other the inscription *"ciel."*

The preceding pictures had dealt with the nonidentity of image and idea (identity cannot be fixed because it exists on the consciousness level only, not on the image level). *On the Threshold of Liberty* makes a different point: the pictures set into the walls indicate the interchangeability of inside and outside, of painting and view, reinforced by the cannon in the room. Magritte was to return to this kind of paradox, which has since become one of his trademarks. *In Praise of Dialectic* (1937) shows an open window through which we look in from outside—at the outer facade of a building.

While Magritte's pictures are often mystifying and enigmatic, they never deal with visions or dreams. They always are the result of pictorial reflections: "The word 'dream' is often misused concerning my painting. We certainly wish the realm of dreams to be respectable—but our works are not oneiric. *On the contrary.* If 'dreams' are concerned in this context, they are very different from those we have while sleeping. It is a question rather of *self-willed* 'dreams' in which nothing is as vague as those feelings one has when escaping in dreams. . . . 'Dreams' which are not intended to make you sleep but to wake you up" (bibl. 115).

On another occasion Magritte said that in his painting there was "no precedence of the unseen over the seen." In this respect Magritte differed from those Surrealists who tried to articulate the unconscious in their pictures. Not personal experience interested him, but pictorial knowledge; he wanted to "wake you up."

Colorplate 27

RENE MAGRITTE

The Human Condition, I

Painted in 1934
Oil on canvas, 39 3/8 × 31 1/2"
Collection Claude Spaak, Choisel, France

"I placed in front of a window, seen from inside a room, a painting representing exactly that part of the landscape which was hidden from view by the painting. Therefore, the tree represented in the painting hid from view the tree situated behind it, outside the room. It existed for the spectator, as it were, simultaneously in his mind, as both inside the room in the painting, and outside in the real landscape" (Magritte, "Lifeline," in *View,* VII, 2, 1946).

In the late 1920s, Magritte began to develop a series of picture problems, one of which we see in *The Human Condition, I:* the relationship between a picture and that which it depicts. Magritte produced a number of such paintings about painting: three different versions of *The Beautiful Captive* (1931, 1935, and 1947), *The Human Condition, II* (1935), *L'Appel des cimes* (1942), and *The Promenades of Euclid* (1955). Earlier pictures, too, had tentatively dealt with that theme. It is to be assumed that Magritte was influenced by De Chirico, who also used the picture within the picture as outside view.

In *The Human Condition, I,* Magritte made use of a landscape motif which, in itself, is not particularly distinguished, in order to deal with the subject of the representation of reality in a picture. Reality, when turned into image—thus placed in a different medium with different laws—loses its reality character and becomes a symbol which points to reality or to a part of reality. One difference in medium is that the image is two-dimensional while reality is three-dimensional. Even the most painstaking image is not that which it represents but merely a symbol for it. "And being a symbol means that image and object are separate and nonidentical, though identity is indicated and felt (in our consciousness)" (H. H. Holz, "Kritische Theorie des ästhetischen Zeichens," Kat. *documenta 5,* Kassel, 1972).

Magritte recognized this nonidentity, while his pictures pretend identity. In *The Human Condition, I,* motif and image have become identical, but of course this is the case only because both are within the painting: the difference in level is cancelled because both are subject to the laws of the painting in which they appear. A seemingly simple painting—of a picture in front of a landscape which represents that landscape—becomes an extremely complex comment on the relation between image and reality. We become aware of this complexity as soon as we begin putting it into words.

But in *The Human Condition, I,* Magritte dealt not only with the dialectical answer to the question of nonidentity of image and subject, of symbol and meaning, but also with a certain approach to art that regards a picture as a window through which we look (for instance, at reality). On the one hand, Magritte seemed to confirm this notion; he pretended that the picture within the picture can be seen through, like a window. On the other hand, there is no getting around the fact that the picture in the picture stands in our way of seeing the view from the window. In other words, the picture partially replaces the window: the picture may be a window but the view through the window also appears as a picture. There seems to be a kind of interchangeability between inside and outside, between what is near and what is distant. Magritte himself has commented on this (in the quotation given above) by pointing out that a part of the landscape, most noticeably the tree, has been brought into the room, although it is outside and exists as an outside (and especially a *real*) tree in the mind of the viewer.

This kind of ambivalence, treated with veristic technique, is as much part of Surrealist painting as is the intellectual approach which we also find (though in different forms) in the works of Max Ernst and Man Ray. If we regard Duchamp as the prototype of the scandalous, Man Ray the prototype of the inventive, and Max Ernst the prototype of the inspirative artist, in the twentieth century, then Magritte would certainly have to be called the prototype of the intellectual artist. None of these men was concerned with "art" as such for its own sake, although their scandals and inventions and inspirative experiments and philosophic reflections have become accepted as works of art because they appear in the guise of pictures or aesthetic objects.

Magritte simply felt he could communicate his ideas best through the medium of painting: "Painting is merely a means to an end for me; it allows me to describe an idea which is produced solely by what the world of the visible has to offer" (bibl. 113).

Colorplate 28

RENE MAGRITTE

Perspective: Madame Récamier by David

Painted in 1951
Oil on canvas, 24 1/4 × 32 1/8"
Private collection

In 1930, Magritte—whose artistic approach remained the same all his life, except for a brief period during World War II—did two adaptations of famous earlier works of art: *Madame Récamier,* after Jacques-Louis David's painting of 1800, and *The Balcony* (1868), after Manet. To the Surrealists, any picture was fair game, whether it was a poster, a magazine illustration, or the work of a great artist of the past.

David's canvas is unfinished, rather freely painted, and quite large (5'7" × 7'10 1/2"). Magritte has reduced David's picture in size and has used a much tighter technique. He has replaced Madame Récamier with a coffin bent at an angle, which imitates the lady's reclining pose. The surprise element lies in the fact that the human figure which we expect to see has been changed into an object that seems to have nothing at all in common with her. This object, the coffin, proclaims the death of Madame Récamier, who—for the viewer familiar with David's picture—is definitely alive. In Magritte's version of *The Balcony,* Manet's three figures are also replaced by coffins.

This linking of incongruous elements, which seems especially striking in *Madame Récamier by David,* gives rise to the question whether Magritte would have accepted any kind of irrational combination. But this is not the case. Somebody once suggested to Magritte that he paint a Venus de Milo made of colored stone. His answer was extremely enlightening:

> I don't quite see the point of a Venus made of multicolored granite: since she is already made of stone, I feel that a more accurate description of a specific kind of stone would add nothing to our knowledge that the statue is made of stone. This type of specification belongs, in my opinion, in the realm of geology; it removes us from the poetic feeling that stems from our knowledge of the mysterious existence of stone. This feeling would be intensified, however, if the Venus de Milo were shown as a statue made of flesh: the unexpected absence of the stone in a place where stone exists in reality and, conversely, the presence of the form which that stone represents, would have to create the mystery. The "nature" of such a statue would not be arbitrary, nor is this a matter of whim: she must be made of flesh. A Venus de Milo made of wood, multicolored granite, aluminum, straw, or any other material would not transcend the realm of fantasy or accidental whim (letter, 1965; bibl. 113).

Thus, the linking of incongruous elements cannot be arbitrary; in order to be convincing and enigmatic, it must be based on a leap of logic and not on the kind of accident that played so important a part in the work of Max Ernst.

Magritte derived his principle of systematic combination from a personal experience that contained the key elements of night (dream) and bird, and whose seminal character is not unlike certain experiences described in the biographies of Leonardo (as analyzed by Freud), James Ensor, and Ernst.

> One night in 1936, I awoke in a room where a cage and the bird sleeping in it had been placed. A magnificent error caused me to see an egg in the cage instead of the bird. I then grasped a new and astonishing poetic secret, because the shock I experienced had been provoked precisely by the affinity of two objects, the cage and the egg, whereas previously I used to provoke this shock by bringing together objects that were unrelated. Even after that revelation I sought to discover if objects other than the cage could not likewise manifest—by bringing to light some element peculiar to them and rigorously predetermined—the same evident poetry that the conjunction of the egg and the cage had suceeded in producing. . . . Since this research could yield only one single exact response for each object, my investigations resembled the pursuit of the solution to a problem for which I had three data: the object, the thing connected with it in the shadow of my consciousness, and the light wherein that thing would become apparent (bibl. 114).

The enigmatic quality of these pictures—Magritte himself always referred to their "mystery"—is thus neither accidental, nor is it the result of irrational content. The enigma is produced deliberately; in order to present it, Magritte utilizes the methods of combination, metamorphosis, and semantics.

Colorplate 29

RENE MAGRITTE

Ready-Made Bouquet

Painted in 1957

Oil on canvas, 62 5/8 × 50 5/8"

Collection Mr. and Mrs. Barnet Hodes, Chicago

The Surrealists felt free to make use of any picture, whether it was taken from an advertisement, an old magazine, or a museum. Duchamp put a mustache on the *Mona Lisa.* Max Ernst subverted Parmigianino's *Madonna with the Long Neck* with his *Blessed Virgin Chastising the Infant Jesus* (1926), and echoed Grünewald in his *Temptation of Saint Anthony* (1945); Man Ray utilized Ingres; Dali transformed the Venus de Milo into an object with bureau drawers and changed the meaning of Millet's *Angelus;* Magritte translated well-known images by Manet and David (see colorplate 28). At times, the Surrealist artists have also quoted each other. Max Ernst borrowed De Chirico's head of a father, as did Dali somewhat later (figs. 14–15 and colorplate 19). In the late twenties, Magritte repeatedly used a framed naked female torso which Delvaux was to adopt and which Duchamp used in a picture titled *In the Manner of Delvaux* (1942); Dali, too, has utilized it (colorplate 24).

There are other instances of such direct and satirical references, and there are also more hidden allusions. The alteration of an old picture almost always represents an act of provocation and "desecration."

Magritte's picture *Ready-Made Bouquet* gets its mysterious tension from the Renaissance "quote" which the artist has attached to the man's back: the figure of Flora from Botticelli's *Primavera.* Smaller in scale than the man, this figure looks (and is meant to look) like a small-sized reproduction and not a part of the picture itself.

The simple picture content—a man looking into a forest across a stone balustrade—is destroyed by the introduction of a graceful female figure. Besides, there is a contradiction between what the figure symbolizes (spring) and the season indicated by the forest (summer). Magritte is not altering a situation or a person into something else in this picture; he is adding a preformed element to an otherwise unequivocal image: the picture becomes ambivalent through the collage-like addition. The contrast between these two elements is neither softened nor explained; it simply exists.

The man in the bowler hat appears often in Magritte's later work. He is usually seen with his face turned away, or else the face is replaced by some other object; the man remains anonymous. The fact that Magritte had himself photographed several times wearing a bowler hat and a black coat allows us to regard the man in the bowler hat as a self-portrait. However, unlike most of the other Surrealists, Magritte abhorred all forms of publicity or notoriety. He led the life of an unremarkable, ordinary citizen. This withdrawal into harmless anonymity also is typical of the men in bowler hats in his pictures. If we regard them as self-portraits we do so for the very reason that they show only general, unremarkable features, that they refuse to yield any information about character or personality and thus leave us, the spectators, helplessly behind.

Colorplate 30

RENE MAGRITTE

The Domain of Arnheim

Painted in 1962
Oil on canvas, 57 7/8 × 44 7/8″
Collection Mme René Magritte, Brussels

In 1949 Magritte painted a window flanked by curtains, through whose partially shattered glass a snowy mountain range can be seen; one of the mountain peaks has the shape of a bird's head. The fallen glass splinters are puzzle-like pieces of the same view. The picture's title, *The Domain of Arnheim,* was derived from a tale by Edgar Allan Poe.

In 1962 the artist created a different version of *The Domain of Arnheim,* this time without the window and without the motif of interchangeability of inside and outside. The theme of the newer picture is the metamorphosis of a mountain into a bird. In a gouache version of 1950, the nest on the stone balustrade is missing; in its place there is a burning candle. The same motif, combined with other elements, recurs in 1951–53 as part of the large-scale mural panels for the casino in Knokke-Le Zoute.

This picture, too, contains paradoxes and incongruous combinations. The bird and its wings are part of the mountain, and yet it is a bird, though covered with snow, like the rock. The nest with its three eggs (which are definitely not made of stone) indicates that the bird is real. What else are we to guess than that the bird has laid those eggs—the bird that is made of stone identical to the rock of the mountain.

A blue daytime sky stands above the mountain, and the entire mountain has taken on the same shade of blue. But, instead of the sun, there is a sickle moon in that bright sky.

The elements of mountain, bird, nest, daylight, and moon are unequivocal. But, in the context of the picture they have become equivocal, because the picture indicates daylight and at the same time insists that it is night; it shows a bird which is stone, but which has laid real eggs.

In his later work, Magritte often has figures turned into stone. Sometimes entire rooms or groups of people are stone. But we must be careful not to put a metaphysical or existential interpretation on these metamorphoses. Magritte himself once wrote that his pictures did not try to hide anything visible, much less anything invisible. Many aspects of his earlier works, such as the pair of boots that terminate in flesh-colored toes (*The Red Model,* 1935), or the figure with the head and chest of a fish and the lower torso of a woman—a kind of mermaid in reverse (*The Collective Invention,* 1934)—indicate that the only thing that mattered to Magritte was the pleasure of performing *post-facto* metamorphoses and the irritation this produced in the spectator.

Rationally applied metamorphosis was just one of several methods this Belgian Surrealist employed in the creation of his seemingly simple yet profoundly mysterious pictures. Their mystery is the result of very precise artistic calculation.

Colorplate 31

PABLO PICASSO (1881–1973)

Painter and His Model

Painted in 1928

Oil on canvas, 51 1/8 × 65 1/8"

The Museum of Modern Art, New York City. Harriet and Sidney Janis Collection

To call Picasso a Surrealist would certainly be a misinterpretation. His art cannot be so narrowly categorized. Besides, Picasso never became a member of the Surrealist group, though several of its members tried very hard to win him over. Still, Picasso did take part in several important Surrealist group exhibitions: at the Galerie Pierre in Paris in 1925; at the Galerie Goemans in Paris, 1930; at the Wadsworth Atheneum, Hartford, Connecticut, in 1931; at the Julien Levy Gallery in New York, 1932; and at the Galerie Charles Ratton in Paris, and The Museum of Modern Art in New York in 1936. He also wrote a few poems in the thirties which were based on Surrealist (meaning, in this case, automatic) principles. This is why the *Dictionnaire abrégé du surréalisme* has this entry for Picasso: "Painter whose work partakes objectively of Surrealism since 1926. Author of Surrealist poems (1935–1938)."

All of Picasso's work was based on a continuing dialogue with the world around him and with the artistic avant-garde of the particular period. Since the Surrealists were more concerned with creating an interior world than in commenting on the world around them, Picasso's art does not fit their program. But his sensitivity to the prevailing artistic climate of the period was bound to bring him under the influence of the Surrealists, and we can see this especially in the work he did about 1930. Thus, while his basic attitude differed sharply from that of the Surrealists, there are nevertheless certain points of contact which justify a discussion of the Surrealist aspects of his work of that time. Nor is the fact to be overlooked that throughout and beyond the twenties, Picasso exerted a strong influence on the Surrealists, among whom he had several good friends.

The artist and his model was a favorite motif for Picasso since the late twenties, when he had illustrated Balzac's *Le Chef-d'oeuvre inconnu* (1927). We find this subject in many variations—in his paintings, drawings, and prints—and he remained involved with it to the end of his life. Whereas Max Ernst, in his Loplop series, tried to establish an ironic distance between himself and his work, Picasso wholeheartedly embraced the contemplation of his own artistic activity. Actually, the motif of artist and model is metaphorical, since Picasso usually worked without a model. What matters is the pictorial reflection on his own person and creative activity. At times the subject seems to serve the glorification of the female nude, but at others it appears to be an encoded message about the process by which reality is turned into a work of art.

The relatively large painting shown here demonstrates such a message. Here, all the elements we can identify as representing reality are turned into an abstract pattern. The painter (at the right) is painting the model's face. And on the canvas that face is far more realistic than that of the "model" who has been subjected to a quasi-Cubist transformation. Picasso's transfer of reality into a work of art and the resulting subordination of reality to the laws of the picture seem to have been playfully reversed on the canvas in the center of the picture.

Colorplate 32

PABLO PICASSO

Bathers Playing Ball

Painted in 1932

Oil on canvas, 57 1/2 × 44 7/8"

Collection Mr. and Mrs. Victor Ganz, New York City

From 1927 on, Picasso drew three-dimensional figures that looked like monstrous pieces of sculpture rather than women. Tanguy's sculpture landscapes may well have served as models. The Verism of the Improbable shows up in Picasso's work in several different forms: in the statues he designed in Dinard, in his various bathing scenes, and in *An Anatomy* (fig. 48). At that same time, nonexistent creatures also appeared in the work of Max Ernst and, somewhat later, Victor Brauner, André Masson, and Oscar Dominguez similarly pictorialized unreal objects. This aspect of Surrealism led to certain misunderstandings. The fantastic or improbable object as such is not Surrealistic. It must express the search for a way to say something that has not yet been said in pictures that speak simultaneously to the unconscious and the rational mind, without necessarily softening or eliminating whatever contradictions might arise. Max Ernst's *An Ear Lent* of 1935, which derives from his *Monument to Birds* (1927), has a certain sculptural quality not unlike that in Picasso's *Bathers Playing Ball.*

The Bathers and *Women on the Beach,* which Picasso painted about 1930, are enormously simplified pneumatic shapes, evolved from the sturdily voluptuous women of his classicist style. Like Tanguy's biomorphic shapes, they replace the reality of a likeness with the reality of an invented picture. This is a somewhat unusual departure for Picasso and can probably be traced to the Surrealists' influence on his work during that period. These pictures reflect the general interest in artificial figures of various kinds that prevailed at the time.

Picasso's drawings made in Cannes and Dinard were meant as designs for monuments and, indeed, it is easy to imagine these ball-playing bathers translated into some sort of heroic sculpture.

Colorplate 33

OSCAR DOMINGUEZ (1906–1957)

Electrosexual Sewing Machine

Painted in 1934
Oil on canvas, 39 3/8 × 31 5/8″
Galerie F. A. Petit, Paris

At the beginning of the thirties, the Paris group of Surrealists was enlarged by the arrival of several new artists. Each one brought his own ideas and techniques; thus the spectrum of Surrealism was broadened while its basic premises remained unchanged. From Rumania came Victor Brauner and Jacques Hérold; from Germany Hans Bellmer, Richard Oelze, and Méret Oppenheim; Wolfgang Paalen came from Austria, and Kurt Seligmann from Switzerland.

In this new generation of artists, all born within the first decade of the twentieth century, Oscar Dominguez must be counted too. He was born in 1906 in the Canary Islands. When he came to Paris in 1934 and made contact with the Surrealists there, he had already participated in a Surrealist exhibition in Tenerife. In Paris, he painted his first pictures containing figures. Somewhat later, he created his partly nonobjective decalcomanias (fig. 57) and several Surrealist objects. He took part in many of the subsequent Surrealist exhibitions, especially the 1936 show at the Galerie Charles Ratton in Paris, at which mainly objects by members of the movement were exhibited, most of them created specifically for that exhibition.

Dominguez's *Electrosexual Sewing Machine* is based on the principle of combining nonrelated elements, a principle which Lautréamont had put into words when he remarked on the beauty of an accidental encounter between an umbrella and a sewing machine on an operating table. The combination of unrelated but accurately depicted recognizable objects—a woman's body, a funnel—is augmented by the addition of pictorial elements that are completely unrecognizable and give no clue as to their function or the material they are made of. The pictorial practices of Max Ernst and Tanguy are both present here. The three-dimensional representation of deliberately enigmatic elements, which culminated in the paintings of Dali, enjoyed a certain vogue with the Surrealist painters of the thirties: not only with Dominguez but also with Picasso, Max Ernst (in some of his series), André Masson, and the Danish painter Wilhelm Freddie (*War Monument,* 1936). It is a component of late Surrealism which insists on replacing the reality of that which is depicted by the reality of the picture itself.

Therefore, this kind of picture need not and cannot be explained. The enigmatic appearance is not the result of a complicated train of thought hiding some mysterious meaning. Rather, it is the product of a working method that relates disparate picture elements to each other, or permits them to flow into each other. It is nothing more; meaning and image are not identical and whatever has been mysteriously arrived at must remain mysterious and inexplicable—not out of respect for the artist's deeper intentions but because mystification is the very principle of the picture.

While Dominguez, in his *Electrosexual Sewing Machine,* eschews the kind of photographically precise method practiced by Tanguy, his picture does contain shapes giving a definitely three-dimensional illusion. The late thirties saw a flowering of Surrealist objects: inspired by Duchamp and Man Ray as well as by Max Ernst's and Kurt Schwitters's Dada inventions, bizarre and grotesque objects were created that made up the largest part of Ratton's 1936 exhibition: Roland Penrose's *Last Voyage of Captain Cook,* Max Ernst's *Object for Family Use,* Wilhelm Freddie's *Sex-Paralysappeal,* Hans Bellmer's *Doll,* Maurice Henry's *Homage to Paganini,* Méret Oppenheim's *Fur-Covered Cup, Saucer, and Spoon* (fig. 60), Dali's *Aphrodisiac Jacket,* Joan Miró's *Poetic Object* (all 1936), as well as Oscar Dominguez's *The Peregrinations of Georges Hugnet* (1935) and *The Coming of the Belle Epoque* (1936).

At the International Surrealist Exhibition at the Galerie des Beaux-Arts in Paris in 1938, the single objects had grown into environments. All members of the Surrealist group developed spatial projects of extreme irrationality which—in spite of their intended "symbolic function"—were aimed first of all at baffling and irritating the viewer. In addition to Dali's *Rainy Taxi* (fig. 66) and a large number of window dummies, garbed or physically altered in various ways by the Surrealists, the show also contained an object by Dominguez which continued along the line of his paintings: a pair of woman's legs emerges from the horn of an old-fashioned gramophone and a woman's breast lies on its turntable.

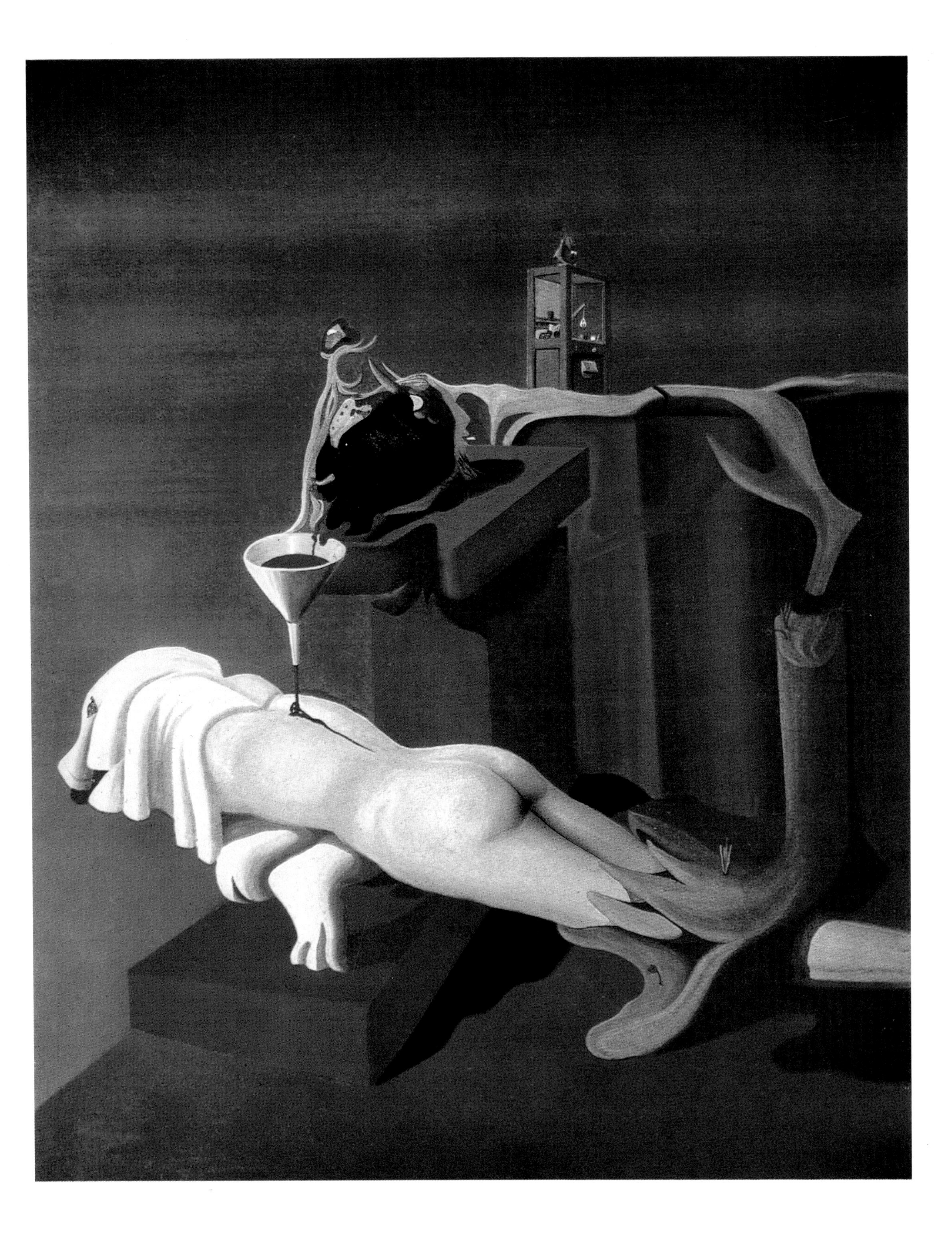

Colorplate 34

MAN RAY (b. 1890)

Imaginary Portrait of D. A. F. de Sade

Painted in 1940
Oil on canvas, 20 × 16"
Private collection

Man Ray, born in Philadelphia in 1890, started out as a painter. In 1915 he began to work with photography. About 1917 he established a kind of New York branch of Dada, together with Duchamp and Picabia (creating, among other things, the first décollages); in 1918 he developed his aerographs, in 1920 he made one of the first kinetic objects (*Lampshade*). Also in 1920, he founded the Société Anonyme with Katherine Dreier and Duchamp and created the first example of packaged art, *The Enigma of Isidore Ducasse* (fig. 62). In 1921 he created the first Rayographs, and he was also accepted into the Dada circle in Paris. In 1923 he made his first film, *Le Retour à la raison;* in 1924 he appeared, with Duchamp and Erik Satie, in *Entr'acte* (a film sequence in the ballet *Relâche*) by Picabia and René Clair; in 1925 he took part in the first Surrealist group exhibition in the Galerie Pierre in Paris; in 1926 he worked with Duchamp and Marc Allégret on the film *Anemic Cinema* and in 1927 made a film of his own, *Emak Bakia,* followed up with *L'Etoile de mer* in 1928 and *Les Mystères du château de dé* in 1929. In addition, he made numerous photographs of his contemporaries (figs. 19 and 55), numerous drawings, Dada and Surrealist objects (among them *The Gift,* 1921—a flatiron with a row of nails sticking out of its plate). In 1932 he was represented—along with Dali, Ernst, Picasso, and Pierre Roy—in a Surrealist exhibition at the Julien Levy Gallery in New York, and in 1936 at the Surrealist exhibitions at the New Burlington Galleries in London and at The Museum of Modern Art in New York.

Man Ray is an inventor and inspirer who had a tremendous influence on Dada and Surrealism, without having been an active, important member of either movement for any length of time. He is a peripheral figure in the Surrealist movement; nevertheless, he took part in all its most important exhibitions and, in 1926, the opening exhibition at the Galerie Surréaliste in Paris was dedicated to his work. Man Ray's witty contributions to painting, drawing, object creation, motion pictures, and photography are—very much in keeping with the ideas of Surrealism—absolutely disparate in style. What they do have in common is the search for ever-new inventions, the continual effort to destroy artistic conventions, and to find new ways of expression (not excluding the joke or prank).

Among Man Ray's comparatively few paintings is his *Imaginary Portrait of D. A. F. de Sade,* of which there exist a 1936 sketch and an earlier painted version dated 1938. The Marquis de Sade was highly regarded as a model worthy of imitation by the Surrealists. His glorification of evil, lust, and sexuality, and his rebellion against traditional values all make him the prototype of the Surrealist man.

Before being locked away in an insane asylum at Charenton (where he stayed until his death), he spent years in various French prisons, including the Bastille. In 1789, at the start of the French Revolution, the Bastille, symbol of absolute monarchy, was stormed by the people. It was razed and its stones were used to build a bridge across the Seine.

Man Ray, in this picture, connects the razing of the Bastille with a monument to the Marquis de Sade that seems to be built from the stones of the wrecked fortress. The Marquis is simultaneously a piece of sculpture and a seemingly living portrait. The use of bricks or stones in sculpture calls to mind Bellmer's similar combinations (mainly in portraits) and anticipates the stone metamorphoses of Magritte's later work.

Man Ray's Marquis de Sade is a heroic monument to the revered ancestor of the Surrealist movement. The reference to the destruction of the Bastille as the stronghold of arbitrary power also indicates the revolutionary role in which the Surrealists had cast the Marquis.

Colorplate 35

RICHARD OELZE (b. 1900)

Expectation

Painted in 1935
Oil on canvas, 32 1/8 × 39 5/8″
The Museum of Modern Art, New York City

On a wooded hillside under a lowering sky stands a group of people, most of them with their backs to the viewer. We can tell from the angle of their heads that they are looking up at the sky. The light is pale and ghostly, and we can't determine its source. The group is lighted from behind, and a clump of trees in the middle ground, at the right, is also illuminated.

The technique with which this picture is painted might be classified as realistic. But Oelze uses this veristic approach in order to make mystery—an element we encounter again and again in Surrealist pictures—the real subject of his painting. Any kind of guess or attempt at interpretation, such as the question of who or what is being expected, would be wrong. The picture presents a situation and leaves it open. It declines to answer the question about the purpose of this waiting. If we think of Max Ernst as an artist who used inspirative techniques, we might regard Oelze as one who worked with inspirative contents.

Oelze was born in Magdeburg, Germany, in 1900. From 1921 to 1925 he studied at the Bauhaus in Weimar, where he took part in its 1923 exhibition. After spending several years in Dresden, Ascona, and Berlin, he found himself in Paris where, in 1932, he maintained a casual contact with the Surrealists. In 1936 he took part in the Surrealist exhibitions in London (New Burlington Galleries) and New York (The Museum of Modern Art). The same year he broke off his stay in Paris, traveled for several years, and then became a prisoner of war. In 1946 he returned to West Germany.

His later works, while quite dissimilar in technique to decalcomania, have this in common with it: they develop heads and eyes metamorphically out of diffuse structures which then often turn into landscapes or forests.

Colorplate 36

HANS BELLMER (b. 1902)

Peppermint Tower in Honor of Greedy Little Girls

Painted in 1942
Oil on canvas, 38 1/8 × 35"
Private collection

Bellmer was born in Katowice, Poland, in 1902. Like De Chirico and Dali, he fell under the spell of Böcklin, and like De Chirico and Ernst, he was impressed by Max Klinger. While studying at the technical college in Berlin (1923–24) he met George Grosz, John Heartfield, and Rudolf Schlichter. He broke off his studies in order to design book jackets and illustrations for Wieland Herzfelde's left-wing publishing house, Malik-Verlag, in Berlin. From 1924 to 1925 he lived in Paris. In 1933 he decided not to produce any work that might, even indirectly, benefit Nazi Germany. He began working on his *Doll,* got in touch with the Paris Surrealists, developed his first objects and, in 1938, moved to Paris and renounced his German citizenship. Before the thirties were over, he had taken part in most of the important Surrealist shows.

Bellmer's central theme is the Doll; during the thirties he produced several objects, all of which were versions of his Doll: there is one dated 1934 (fig. 63), another dated 1936, and one titled *The Machine-Gunneress,* produced in 1937. The doll is Bellmer's symbol for his own psychic conflicts in respect to his childhood and the child-woman eroticism that obsessed him. It is partly derived from the articulated dolls of Albrecht Dürer's time which Bellmer saw in the Kaiser Friedrich Museum in Berlin and partly from the character of Olympia in one of E.T.A. Hoffmann's stories.

Bellmer's extensive oeuvre includes a number of gouaches from the time when decalcomania was in vogue, but, most important, a wealth of extremely delicate drawings, which toward the end of the thirties took on a collage-like quality. Many of them include the articulated limbs and ball joints of the dolls (fig. 64). Bellmer produced his first version of *Peppermint Tower in Honor of Greedy Little Girls* in 1936, the same year he made a doll that can be called a visual counterpart to the palindrome: this doll can be stood on its head, and still look the same, for the breasts and buttocks are identical in both halves.

Through Freud, the Surrealists were familiar with the repression of sexual drives. In Bellmer's work, these drives become explicit. In his later drawings, he demonstrated the equivalence of body openings: eye, ear, and mouth are the same as vagina and anus, and he also coupled thighs and breasts, penis and leg, knee and glans. Bellmer himself once described this principle: "How, indeed, could one depict—without impoverishing—the inner scheme of a little girl who sits and dreams with her left shoulder pulled up and her arms extended, languidly leaning across a table, concealing the instinctive caress of her chin between shoulder and pectoral muscle, so that the weight of the head is added to that of shoulder and arm, a pressure that is reflected in the counterpressure from the tabletop which runs along the muscles in diminishing strength, stops briefly at the elbow, then passes, weaker still, over the slightly raised wrist and, in a final drop, slides down the back of the hand and terminates between the index finger and the tabletop in the pointed shape of a small sugar cone? . . . As soon as the intuitive position of the chin has indicated an analogy between sex organ and armpit, the images become superimposed, mixed in content. The sex organ is projected onto the armpit, the foot on the hand, toes on fingers. And there arises a peculiar mixture of the real and the imagined, of the permissible and the forbidden aspects of the two components" (*Die Puppe,* Berlin, 1962).

What we encounter in this picture is a modification of the Surrealist method of incongruous combination. In place of a juxtaposition of completely disparate elements, we find elements that are related in content but put together in new and unexpected ways. This brings to mind another word game, the game of anagrams, in which all the letters of a certain word are put together in a different sequence to form a new word. By this method, André Breton transformed the name "Salvador Dali" into "Avida Dollars," a pointed reference to Dali's interest in money. Bellmer himself alludes to this in an essay called *Petite Anatomie de l'inconscient physique ou l'anatomie de l'image* (Paris, 1957), in which he remarks: "The human body can be compared to a sentence we want to take apart in order to re-create its true meaning through an infinite series of anagrams."

Bellmer's anagrammatical principle fits in perfectly with Surrealist methods of picture-making. In *Peppermint Tower* he merely hints at this principle. The figure in the background reflects Magritte's stone metamorphoses. That in the foreground is reminiscent of Dali's *Cannibalism in Autumn* (colorplate 23) and deals explicitly with sexual meanings that appear disguised in Dali's pictures. The attack on traditional taboos which the Surrealists demanded as early as the twenties is expressed clearly, wittily, and with sovereign pictorial virtuosity by Bellmer.

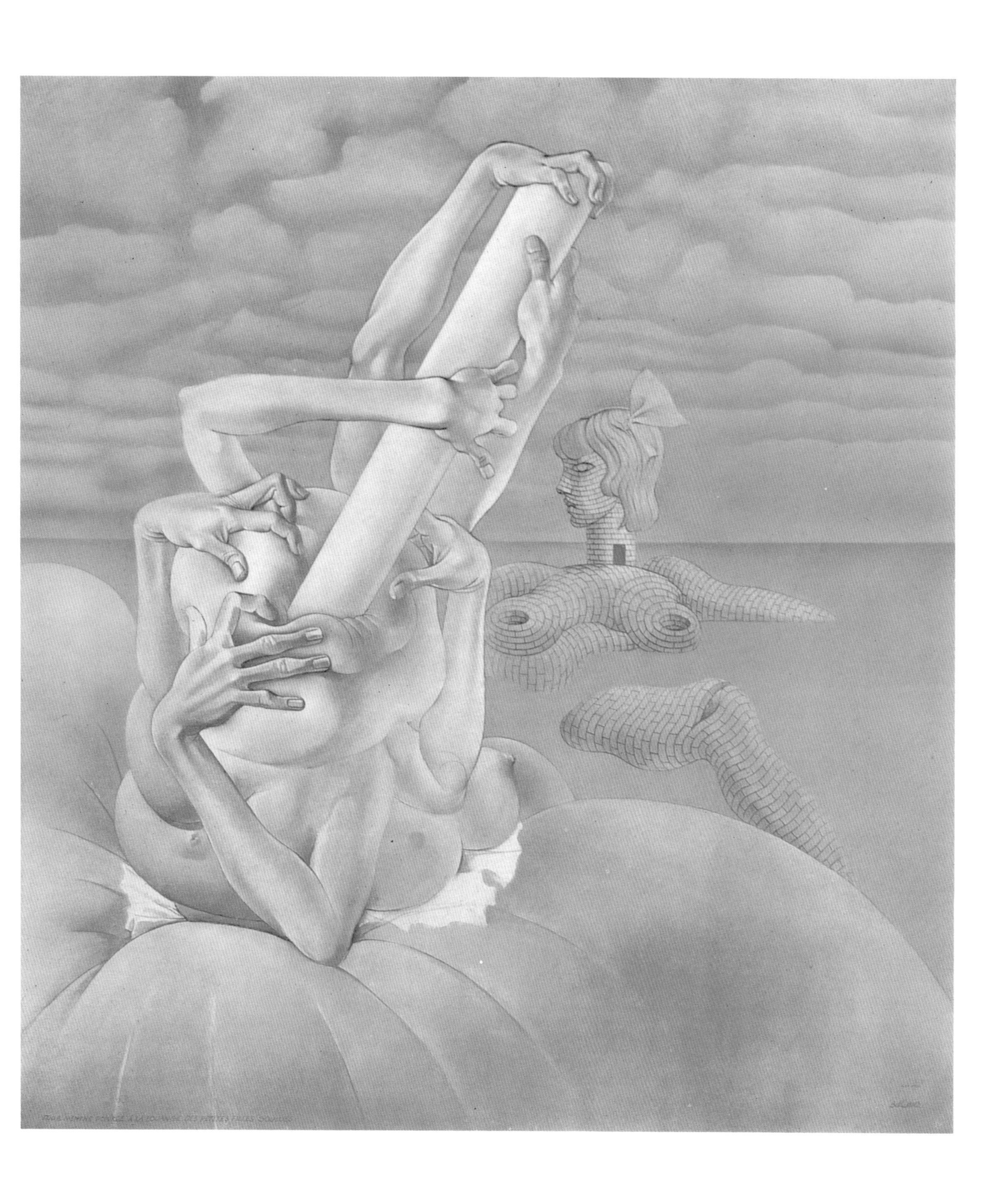

Colorplate 37

PAUL DELVAUX (b. 1897)

Pygmalion

Painted in 1939
Oil on wood, 53 1/8 × 65"
Musées Royaux des Beaux-Arts de Belgique, Brussels

In 1937, Paul Delvaux joined the group of Belgian Surrealists around René Magritte and E. L. T. Mesens. Delvaux was born in Antheit in 1897. He studied at the Académie des Beaux-Arts in Brussels from 1920 to 1924. Until 1930, he was strongly influenced by Belgian Expressionist painting. The avant-garde of this time did not particularly attract him. But, in 1934, there was an exhibition in Brussels at which works by De Chirico, Dali, and Magritte were shown. This made such a strong impression on Delvaux that his painting began to take a turn toward Surrealism, and his pictures became progressively more Surrealist in character. In 1938, he took part in the *Exposition Internationale du Surréalisme* in the Galerie des Beaux-Arts in Paris. Delvaux's work, like Magritte's, changed only minimally in the course of the decades that followed. His motifs were naked women, skeletons, classical architecture, railroad stations, trains; his themes were love, death, longing. The picture is a stage with *fin-de-siècle* props on which the characters are frozen in theatrical poses.

In his early Surrealist work—created when he was forty years old—Delvaux presented all the ingredients of his later pictures but without the schematization he imposed on them later on. In *Pygmalion,* motionlessness is the theme but not yet the principle of the picture.

In the Greek myth, the sculptor Pygmalion falls in love with the statue of a young girl he has just completed. He prays to Aphrodite to give the image life, that it may reciprocate his love. Moved by such devotion, Aphrodite brings the statue to life. Delvaux has reversed the story in his picture and has applied the Surrealist principle of introducing incongruous elements. Pygmalion himself is a stone image (the transformation into a live creature takes place in the left background) and a woman is embracing him. Aphrodite, one of whose emblems is the flower, appears again in the middle ground, right, next to a Magrittesque gentleman in a bowler hat.

Delvaux's picture is characterized by an emptiness that seems derived from De Chirico. The seemingly mysterious reversal of the Pygmalion motif shows that the aim of the picture is not simply to illustrate a Classical myth but to demonstrate or develop the principle of metamorphosis which, in Delvaux's work especially, contains the subtheme of life becoming immobilized through art. As a statue, Pygmalion is insensitive and incapable of love; his communication with the goddess of love has become immobilized in an empty gesture.

Colorplate 38

WOLS (1913–1951)

The Banjo

Painted in 1939
Pen and ink and watercolor on paper, 12 1/2 × 9"
Collection Ernst Fischer, Krefeld, Germany

Wols never actually belonged to the Surrealist movement; his personality always resisted joining any group. But he was undeniably influenced by the circle of painters around André Breton. Wols himself referred to some of his pictures of the late thirties and early forties as "Surrealist compositions."

Alfred Otto Wolfgang Schulze was born in Berlin in 1913. His first love was music. During a stay in Dresden (1919–1932) he made friends with Otto Dix, took photographs, and wanted to study ethnology. In 1932 he felt attracted to the Bauhaus in Berlin, but went instead to Paris, where he wrote, photographed, painted, and played the violin, piano, and banjo. In 1934 he went to Spain, but a year later was expelled for political reasons. Like Bellmer and Max Ernst, he was interned as an enemy alien in France in 1939. During the war, in Cassis and Montélimar, he continued to paint and draw under the most difficult circumstances. By this time, his works had taken on the character of L'Art Informel. After 1945 he lived in various hotels in Paris, supported by friends. His financial situation was catastrophic. Toward the end of the forties he fell ill, but had no money for a hospital. Although a withdrawal cure for severe alcoholism improved his health temporarily, a subsequent case of food poisoning found his body so weakened that he succumbed. Wols died in Paris, aged thirty-eight.

His life had been a continuous process of suffering, intensified by self-destructive tendencies. By comparison, his incessant artistic activity seems an act of liberation. His obsession, his compulsive creativity had its source, as it did in the case of Giacometti, in an incurable sickness of the world—the world which can be cancelled out on the fictitious level of a picture.

About 1940 Wols mainly painted watercolors with Surrealist overtones. Recognizable objects are transformed—in the process of being drawn with a nervous, ticking line—into nonobjective forms which are given a three-dimensional, quasi-realistic character through the addition of color. The weightless, floating quality of these pictures may bring to mind the work of Paul Klee. The transformation of the known into something unknown and unknowable is a Surrealist trait. There is also a resemblance to automatic writing and to the "exquisite corpses," due, perhaps, to the sketchlike quality which gives these pictures by Wols such an intensely subjective character.

In the years that followed, Wols independently made the transition to L'Art Informel, which, just about that same time, was made by the young American Abstract Expressionist painters through their encounter with the Surrealist work of French-exiled artists living in New York.

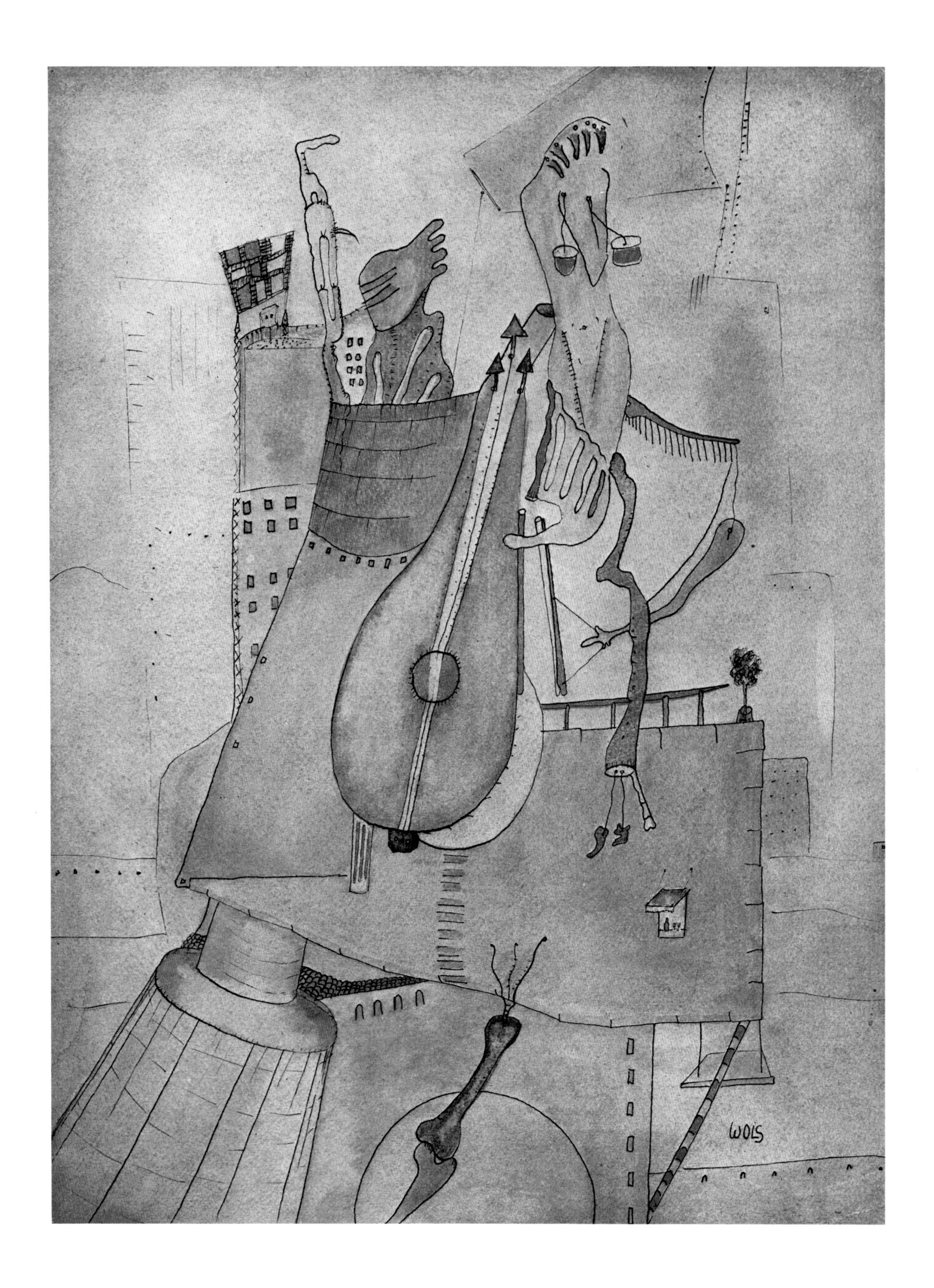
WOLS

Colorplate 39

DOROTHEA TANNING (b. 1913)

The Birthday

Painted in 1942
Oil on canvas, 40 1/8 × 25 5/8"
Collection the artist

Dorothea Tanning was born in Galesburg, Illinois. In 1935 she came to New York, where in 1936 she became acquainted with Surrealism through the big Museum of Modern Art exhibition, *Fantastic Art, Dada and Surrealism*. In 1942, she had a show at the Julien Levy Gallery in New York. Soon afterward, she met Max Ernst and, in 1946, she went to Sedona, Arizona, with him and became his wife. In 1944 Dorothea Tanning showed again at the Julien Levy Gallery and in 1945 she and Max Ernst exhibited jointly at the Crosby Gallery in Washington, D.C.

Dorothea Tanning continues in a vein in which Pierre Roy (colorplate 18) had worked, developing illogical or unlikely combinations of realistic elements. The proliferation of open doors in *The Birthday* conveys a sense of the uncanny, intensified by the figure of the woman and the winged creature in the foreground. We shall never know where these doors lead, or what the woman and the crouching animal are meant to imply or what their purpose or actions intend. The picture poses a riddle and offers no solution; everything has been frozen into immobility. We sense that something extremely disagreeable might be about to happen, but we have no idea what form this menace will take or when it will manifest itself. A deliberately planned enigma is concealed behind a seemingly forthright, realistic technique.

If we wanted to assume that the picture has symbolic significance, we might take it for a self-portrait in which the skirt of many roots points to a closeness to nature while the Renaissance jacket may suggest an affinity with art and with the many Renaissance pictures of Venus. In such a context, the open doors could be interpreted as leading to various new beginnings in the artist's life.

But such a symbolist interpretation of the picture would not be in line with the principles of Surrealist art.

Colorplate 40

ARSHILE GORKY (1904–1948)

Anatomical Wall Chart

Painted in 1943

Pen and ink and chalk, 20 1/4 × 27 3/8''

Collection Mr. and Mrs. Walter Bareiss, New York City

Arshile Gorky was born in Armenia in 1904. In 1943, André Breton, then living in exile in America, discovered his work. He appreciated and sponsored his fellow artist. By the time Gorky had a one-man show at the Julien Levy Gallery in New York in 1945, he was already considered a member of the Surrealist movement.

Gorky's work of the forties points up the decisive change that was taking place in Surrealist art. In the thirties, the dominant trend had been toward a Verism of the Improbable. But the young American painters of the forties, under the influence of earlier Surrealist ideas and techniques, especially those about automatic notation, showed a strong tendency toward spontaneous approaches.

When Arshile Gorky had a retrospective in the San Francisco Museum of Art, he was able to look back on a considerable body of work, including a set of frescoes for Newark Airport (a WPA project, 1935) and for the Airlines Building at the New York World's Fair of 1939. It was only in 1942 that the change in his work took place. Most probably through the influence of Masson and Miró, Gorky developed a L'Art Informel style, although he always worked objective shapes into his pictures. The step toward purely abstract painting remained for Jackson Pollock to take. Gorky is the connecting link between the European Surrealists, whose group he joined as one of the last new members, and the young Americans to whom he demonstrated the actual working of automatism. His influence on these young American artists was enormous. Once again, the activity of producing pictures had become the most important element of art: the center of gravity had shifted from picture content to pictorial process. At the same time, a new phase in art history began—the ascendancy of American contemporary art over European contemporary art.

In 1946 a large part of Gorky's work was destroyed in a studio fire. Two years later, after a severe automobile accident, Arshile Gorky committed suicide.

Colorplate 41

MATTA (b. 1912)

Being There

Painted in 1945–46
Oil on canvas, 7′ 3 3/8″ × 14′ 9 7/8″
Private collection

Matta was born Roberto Sebastián Antonio Matta Echaurren in Santiago, Chile, of Spanish-French parents. In 1934, when he was twenty-two, he went to Paris to study under Le Corbusier. In 1937, he made contact with the Surrealists and the following year he began to paint. At that late period, Surrealism was getting almost no support or impulse from new young artists. Matta is the exception. With Gorky and Robert Motherwell, the two American artists he felt closest to, he constitutes a bridge between the French Surrealists and the younger American painters.

Matta's early pictures have an improvisational quality. Elements of L'Art Informel are interspersed with three-dimensional-looking shapes. At times Matta poured paint directly onto the canvas, then pounded and rubbed it in. Accident played a greater part in his work than plan or intention. His primary interest belonged to the process of picture-making.

More and more, Matta dispensed with spatial indication. There are no horizons in his later pictures. The depth of any given area is completely puzzling, so the viewer never quite knows whether a certain depicted shape is close by or far away. Various objects are placed behind each other and variously illuminated to create a sense of depth, but it is a depth without clear definition or recognizable reality. We are looking into an area in which biomorphic and technoid objects seem to exist in a utopian atmosphere.

Matta himself has said that the only painters who meant anything to him during the period about 1940 were Tanguy and Duchamp. Tanguy's legacy seems to be the creation of a quasi-real pictorial world. With his effects of irregular, indefinable spatial depth; with his oddly shaped creatures placed against a background that seems to indicate a technological world of the future; with his peculiar juxtaposition of technological progress and personal symbols of torture and cruelty (the motif of the mutant being a favorite element of science-fiction literature); with his repertoire of complicated figures and objects spread over a large format, Matta has created an intensely personal, almost poetic pictorial world that contains elements of Surrealism. The real world has become interspersed with an imaginary, threatening world of the future. *Being There,* almost 15 feet long, is the high point and summing-up of this phase of Matta's work, in which menace and aggression become so powerful that one is tempted to draw comparisons with Picasso's *Guernica.*

BIBLIOGRAPHY

DADA

1 Richard Huelsenbeck. *Einleitung zum Dada-Almanach.* Berlin, Erich Reiss Verlag, 1920; reprint: Dada Almanach, New York, Something Else Press, 1966

2 ———. *En avant Dada: Die Geschichte des Dadaismus.* Hanover, Paul Steegemann, 1920; English translation in Robert Motherwell, ed., *The Dada Painters and Poets: An Anthology,* New York, Wittenborn, Schultz, 1951; reprint, New York, George Wittenborn, 1967, pp. 21–48

3 Tristan Tzara. "Conférence sur dada," *Merz,* January 1924, pp. 68–70

4 Hugo Ball. *Die Flucht aus der Zeit.* Munich, Von Duncker und Humboldt, 1927

5 George Grosz. *A Little Yes and a Big No; the Autobiography of George Grosz.* New York, The Dial Press, 1946

6 Robert Motherwell, ed. *The Dada Painters and Poets: An Anthology.* New York, Wittenborn, Schultz, 1951; reprint, New York, George Wittenborn, 1967

7 Willy Verkauf, Marcel Janco, and Hans Bolliger, eds. *Dada. Monograph of a Movement.* New York, George Wittenborn, 1957

8 Düsseldorf. Kunstverein für die Rheinlande und Westfalen. *Dada: Dokumente einer Bewegung.* Exhibition. Catalogue compiled by Karl Heinz Hering and Ewald Rathke. 1958; reprint, New York, Arno Press, 1968

9 Walter Mehring. *Berlin Dada: Eine Chronik mit Photos und Dokumenten.* Zurich, Verlag der Arche, 1959

10 Richard Huelsenbeck. *Dada: Eine literarische Dokumentation.* Reinbek, Rowohlt, 1964

11 Michel Sanouillet. *Dada à Paris.* Paris, J. J. Pauvert, 1965

12 Zurich. Kunsthaus. *Dada. Ausstellung zum 50-jährigen Jubiläum.* Kunsthaus, Zurich, 1966; *Exposition commemorative du cinquantenaire.* Musée National d'Art Moderne, Paris, 1966–67. 2 vols., Zurich, 1966

13 Miklavž Prosenc. *Die Dadaisten in Zürich.* Bonn, H. Bouvier, 1967

14 Hans Richter. *Dada: Art and Anti-Art.* New York, Harry N. Abrams, 1970

15 Georges Hugnet. *L'Aventure Dada, 1916–1922.* New ed., augmented, Paris, Seghers, 1971

16 Lucy R. Lippard, *Dadas on Art.* Englewood Cliffs, New Jersey, Prentice-Hall, 1971

17 Raoul Hausmann. *Am Anfang war Dada.* Steinbach-Giessen, Anabas-Verlag, 1972

COLLAGE AND ASSEMBLAGE

18 New York. The Museum of Modern Art. *The Art of Assemblage.* Exhibition. Catalogue by William C. Seitz. New York, 1961

19 Harriet Janis and Rudi Blesh. *Collage: Personalities, Concepts, Techniques.* Rev. ed., Philadelphia and New York, Chilton, 1967

20 Nuremberg. Institut für moderne Kunst. *Prinzip Collage.* Exhibition. Catalogue by Franz Mon and Heinz Neidel. Neuwied, Luchterhand Verlag, 1968

21 Ingolstadt. Stadttheater. *Die Fotomontage. Geschichte und Wesen einer Kunstform.* Exhibition. Catalogue by Richard Hiepe. Ingolstadt, 1969

22 Herta Wescher. *Collage.* New York, Harry N. Abrams, 1971

23 Berlin. Nationalgalerie. *Metamorphose des Dinges. Kunst und Antikunst, 1910–1970.* Exhibition. Berlin, 1971

24 Willy Rotzler. *Objekt-Kunst. Von Duchamp bis Kienholz.* Cologne, M. DuMont Schauberg, 1972

SURREALISM

25 Zurich. Kunsthaus. *Was ist Surrealismus?* Exhibition. Foreword in catalogue by Max Ernst. Zurich, 1934

26 Julien Levy. *Surrealism.* New York, The Black Sun Press, 1936; reprint, New York, Arno Press, 1968

27 Herbert Read, ed. *Surrealism.* London, Faber & Faber; New York, Harcourt, Brace, 1936; reprint, New York, Praeger, 1972

28 New York. The Museum of Modern Art. *Fantastic Art, Dada and Surrealism.* Exhibition. Catalogue by Alfred H. Barr, Jr. New York, 1937; reprint, New York, Arno Press, 1970

29 Dieter Wyss. *Der Surrealismus; Eine Einführung und Deutung surrealistischer Literatur und Malerei.* Heidelberg, L. Schneider, 1950

30 Jacques Hardé. "The Present State of Studies on Literary Surrealism," *Yearbook of Comparative and General Literature,* IX, 1960, pp. 43–66

31 Yves Duplessis. *Surrealism.* New York, Walker, 1963

32 Adonis Kyrou. *Le Surréalisme au cinéma.* Rev. ed., Paris, Le Terrain Vague, 1963

33 Ferdinand Alquié. *The Philosophy of Surrealism.* Ann Arbor, The University of Michigan Press, 1965; paperback reprint, 1969

34 Anna Balakian. "The Significance of the Surrealist Manifestoes," *L'Esprit créateur,* VI, no. 1, Spring 1966, pp. 3–13

35 Pierre José. *Le Surréalisme.* Lausanne, Editions Rencontre, 1966

36 J. H. Matthews. "Forty Years of Surrealism (1924–1964): a Preliminary Bibliography," *Comparative Literature Studies,* III, 1966, pp. 309–350

37 Patrick Waldberg. *Surrealism.* New York, McGraw-Hill, 1966

38 Marcel Jean. *History of Surrealist Painting.* New York, Grove Press, 1967

39 Maurice Nadeau. *History of Surrealism.* Riverside, New Jersey, Macmillan, 1967

40 André Breton. *Manifestoes of Surrealism.* Ann Arbor, University of Michigan Press, 1969

41 Enrico Crispolti. *Il Surrealismo.* Milan, Fratelli Fabbri, 1969

42 Herbert S. Gershman. *A Bibliography of the Surrealist Revolution in France.* Ann Arbor, University of Michigan Press, 1969

43 William S. Rubin. *Dada and Surrealist Art.* New York, Harry N. Abrams, 1969

44 Sarane Alexandrian. *Surrealist Art.* New York, Praeger, 1970

45 Mary Ann Caws. *The Poetry of Dada and Surrealism: Aragon, Breton, Tzara, Eluard and Desnos.* Princeton, Princeton University Press, 1969

46 Hans Holländer. "Ars inveniendi et investigandi: Zur surrealistischen Methode," *Wallraf-Richartz Jahrbuch,* XXXII, 1970, pp. 193–234

47 Lucy R. Lippard, ed. *Surrealists on Art.* Englewood Cliffs, New Jersey, Prentice-Hall, 1970

48 Peter Bürger. *Der französische Surrealismus. Studien zum Problem der avantgardistischen Literatur.* Frankfurt, Athenäum, 1971

49 Jean Decottignies. "L'Oeuvre surréaliste et l'idéologie," *Littérature,* I, February 1971, pp. 30–47

50 Paul C. Ray. *The Surrealist Movement in England.* Ithaca, New York, Cornell University Press, 1971

51 William Gaunt. *The Surrealists.* London, Thames and Hudson; New York, Putnam, 1972

52 José Vovelle. *Le Surréalisme en Belgique.* Brussels, A. De Roche, 1972

53 André Breton. *Surrealism and Painting.* New York, Harper and Row, 1973

ARP

54 Carola Giedion-Welcker. *Jean Arp.* New York, Harry N. Abrams, 1957

55 Michel Seuphor (pseud. for Ferdinand Louis Berckelaers). *Arp.* New York, Universe Books, 1961

BELLMER

56 Hanover. Kestner-Gesellschaft. *Hans Bellmer.* Exhibition. Hanover, 1967

57 André Pieyre de Mandiargues. *Hans Bellmer: Oeuvre gravé.* Paris, Denoël, 1969

58 Paris. Centre National de l'Art Contemporain. *Hans Bellmer.* Exhibition. Paris, 1971

59 Sarane Alexandrian. *Hans Bellmer.* Paris, Filipacchi, 1971

60 Alex Grall, ed. *Hans Bellmer.* Introduction by Constantin Jelenski. London, Academy Editions, 1972; New York, St. Martin's Press, 1973

BRAUNER

61 Alain Jouffroy. *Brauner.* Paris, G. Fall, 1959

62 Sarane Alexandrian, ed. *Les Dessins magiques de Victor Brauner.* Paris, Denoël, 1965

63 Paris. Musée d'Art Moderne. *Victor Brauner.* Exhibition. Catalogue by Dominique Bozo. Paris, 1972

BRETON

64 Julien Gracq. *André Breton. Quelques aspects de l'écrivain.* Paris, J. Corti, 1966

65 Clifford Browder. *André Breton, Arbiter of Surrealism.* Geneva, Droz, 1967

66 Elisabeth Lenk. *Der springende Narziss. André Bretons poetischer Materialismus.* Munich, Rogner & Bernhard, 1971

67 Gisela Steinwachs. *Mythologie des Surrealismus oder die Rückwandlung von Kultur in Natur. Eine strukturale Analyse von Bretons "Nadja."* Neuwied, Luchterhand Verlag, 1971

BUNUEL

68 Adonis Kyrou. *Luis Buñuel.* New York, Simon & Schuster, 1963

69 Alice Goetz and Helmut W. Banz. *Luis Buñuel. Eine Dokumentation.* Edition sponsored by the Deutschen Filmclubs e. V., Bad Ems, 1965

70 Carlos Rebelledo and Frédéric Grange. *Buñuel.* Paris, Editions Universitaires, 1965

71 Luis Buñuel, *L'Age d'or and Un Chien Andalou.* London, Lorrimer Publishing; New York, Simon & Schuster, 1968

72 Raymond Durgnat. *Luis Buñuel.* London, Studio Vista, 1967; Berkeley, University of California Press, 1968

73 Birgit Hein. *Film im Underground, von seinen An-*

fängen bis zum unabhängigen Kino. Frankfurt, Berlin, Vienna: Ullstein, 1971

DALI

74 New York. The Museum of Modern Art. *Salvador Dali.* Exhibition. Catalogue by James Thrall Soby. Second rev. ed. New York, 1946. First printed under the title: *Paintings, Drawings, Prints: Salvador Dali,* 1941

75 Albert Reynolds Morse. *Catalogue of Works by Salvador Dali in Public Museum Collections.* Cleveland, privately printed for the Reynolds-Morse Foundation, 1956

76 ———. *Dali: A Study of His Life and Works.* Greenwich, Connecticut, New York Graphic Society, 1958

77 Fleur Cowles. *The Case of Salvador Dali.* First American ed., Boston, Little, Brown, 1960

78 Stephen Longstreet, *The Drawings of Dali.* Los Angeles, Borden, 1964

79 Max Gérard. *Salvador Dali.* New York, Harry N. Abrams, 1968

80 Baden-Baden. Staatliche Kunsthalle. *Dali: Gemälde, Zeichnungen, Objekte, Schmuck.* Exhibition. Second rev. ed. Baden-Baden, 1971

81 Robert Descharnes. *The World of Salvador Dali.* New ed., London, Basingstroke, Macmillan, 1972

DE CHIRICO

82 New York. The Museum of Modern Art. *Giorgio de Chirico.* Exhibition. Catalogue by James Thrall Soby. New York, 1955; reprint, New York, Arno Press, 1966 (1968). The first edition of this catalogue was entitled: *The Early Chirico,* New York, Dodd, Mead, 1941

83 Luigi Carluccio. *194 Drawings by Giorgio de Chirico.* New York, Harry N. Abrams, 1969

84 Alfonso Ciranna. *Giorgio de Chirico. Catalogo delle opere grafiche "incisioni e litografia" 1921–1969.* Milan, A. Ciranna, 1969

85 Hanover. Kestner-Gesellschaft. *Giorgio de Chirico.* Exhibition at the Orangerie of the Hannover-Herrenhausen. Hanover, 1970

86 Isabella Far, ed. *Giorgio de Chirico.* New York, Harry N. Abrams, 1970

87 Claudio Bruni & Isabella Far, eds. *Catalogo generale dell'opera di Giorgio de Chirico,* 2 vols. Milan, Electa Editrice, 1971–72. Vol. I: 1908–30; Vol. II: 1931–50

DELVAUX

88 Claude Spaak. *Paul Delvaux.* Antwerp, De Sikkel for the Ministerie van Openbaar Onderwijs, 1948

89 Paul-Aloise de Bock. *Paul Delvaux: L'Homme, le peintre, psychologie d'un art.* Brussels, La Conti, 1967

90 Jacques Meuris. *Sept dialogues avec Paul Delvaux, accompagnés de sept lettres imaginaires.* Paris, Le Soleil Noir, 1971

DOMINGUEZ

91 Leverkusen. Städtisches Museum. *Dominguez.* Exhibition. Leverkusen, Germany, 1967–68

ERNST

92 Patrick Waldberg. *Max Ernst.* Paris, J. J. Pauvert, 1958

93 Cologne. Wallraf-Richartz Museum. *Max Ernst.* Exhibition, Cologne, Wallraf-Richartz Museum, 1962–63; Zurich, Kunsthaus, 1963. Catalogue, second ed., Cologne, 1963

94 John Russell. *Max Ernst, His Life and Work.* London, Thames & Hudson; New York, Harry N. Abrams, 1967

95 "Max Ernst parle avec Robert Lebel," *L'Oeil,* no. 176–177, August–September 1969, pp. 28–37, 44–45

96 Werner Spies. *Max Ernst.* New York, Harry N. Abrams, 1969

97 Stuttgart. Württembergischer Kunstverein. *Max Ernst: Gemälde, Plastiken, Collagen, Frottagen, Bücher.* Exhibition. Catalogue by Uwe M. Schneede. Cologne, 1970

98 Werner Spies. *Max Ernst, 1950–1970: The Return of La Belle Jardinière.* New York, Harry N. Abrams, 1971

99 Uwe M. Schneede. *Max Ernst.* London, Thames & Hudson; New York, Praeger, 1973

GIACOMETTI

100 Ernst Scheidegger, ed. *Alberto Giacometti: Schriften, Fotos, Zeichnungen.* Zurich, Peter Schifferli Verlags AG, 1958

101 Palma Bucarelli. *Giacometti.* Rome, Editalia, 1962

102 Jacques Dupin. *Alberto Giacometti.* Paris, Maeght, 1963

103 Paris. Orangerie des Tuileries. *Alberto Giacometti.* Exhibition. Catalogue, second ed., Paris, 1969

104 Reinhold Hohl. *Alberto Giacometti.* New York, Harry N. Abrams, 1972

GORKY

105 Ethel K. Schwabacher. *Arshile Gorky.* New York, published for the Whitney Museum of American Art by Macmillan, 1957

106 Harold Rosenberg. *Arshile Gorky: the Man, the Time, the Idea.* New York, Horizon, 1962

107 New York. The Museum of Modern Art. *Arshile Gorky.* Exhibition. Catalogue by William C. Seitz. New York, 1962; reprint, New York, Arno Press, 1972

108 Julien Levy. *Gorky.* New York, Harry N. Abrams, 1968

LAM

109 Yvon Taillandier. *Wifredo Lam.* Paris, Denoël, 1970

110 Michel Leiris. *Wifredo Lam.* New York, Harry N. Abrams, 1973

MAGRITTE

111 New York. The Museum of Modern Art. *René Magritte.* Exhibition, The Museum of Modern Art, New York; Rose Art Museum, Brandeis University; Art Institute of Chicago; University Art Museum, University of California, Berkeley; Pasadena Art Museum. Catalogue by James Thrall Soby. New York, The Museum of Modern Art, distributed by Doubleday, 1965

112 Patrick Waldberg. *René Magritte.* New York, Wittenborn, 1965

113 Hanover. Kestner-Gesellschaft. *René Magritte.* Exhibition, Kestner-Gesellschaft, Hanover; Kunsthaus, Zurich. Hanover, 1969

114 Philippe Roberts-Jones. *Magritte: poète visible.* Brussels, Laconti, 1972

115 Suzi Gablik. *Magritte.* Greenwich, Connecticut, New York Graphic Society, 1973

MASSON

116 Michel Leiris and Georges Limbour. *André Masson and His Universe.* Geneva, London, Editions des Trois Collines, 1947

117 Otto Hahn. *Masson.* New York, Harry N. Abrams, 1965

118 Jean-Paul Clébert. *Mythologie d'André Masson.* Geneva, Pierre Cailler, 1971

MATTA

119 William S. Rubin. "Matta," *The Museum of Modern Art Bulletin,* XXV, no. 1, 1957. This issue of the *Bulletin* is devoted to the catalogue of the exhibition held at The Museum of Modern Art; the Walker Art Center, Minneapolis; and the Institute of Contemporary Art, Boston, 1957–58

120 Ursula Schmitt. *Matta: Einführung und Katalog der druckgraphischen Werke im Kunstmuseum Silkeborg.* Silkeborg, Denmark, Kunstmuseum, 1969

MIRO

121 James Johnson Sweeney. "Joan Miró. Comment and Interview," *Partisan Review,* XV, no. 2, February 1948, pp. 206–212

122 New York. The Museum of Modern Art. *Joan Miró.* Exhibition. Catalogue by James Thrall Soby. New York, 1959

123 Jacques Dupin. *Joan Miró, Life and Work.* New York, Harry N. Abrams, 1962

124 Jacques Lassaigne. *Miró: Biographical and Critical Study.* Geneva, Skira, 1963

125 Roland Penrose. *Miró.* London, Thames & Hudson; New York, Harry N. Abrams, 1970

126 Margit Rowell. *Miró.* New York, Harry N. Abrams, 1971

OELZE

127 Hanover. Kestner-Gesellschaft. *Richard Oelze.* Exhibition, Kestner-Gesellschaft, Hanover, 1964; Württembergischer Kunstverein, Stuttgart, 1964–65. Hanover, 1964

OPPENHEIM

128 Stockholm. Moderna Museet. *Méret Oppenheim.* Exhibition. Stockholm, 1967

MAN RAY

129 Los Angeles County Museum of Art. *Man Ray.* Exhibition. Catalogue by Jules Langsner. Los Angeles, 1966

130 Paolo Fossati. *Oggetti d'affezione.* Turin, Einaudi, 1970

131 Rotterdam. Museum Boymans–van Beuningen. *Man Ray.* Exhibition. Rotterdam, 1971

PIERRE ROY

132 Hanover. Kestner-Gesellschaft. *Pierre Roy.* Exhibition. Hanover, 1967

TANGUY

133 André Breton. *Yves Tanguy.* New York, Pierre Matisse, 1946

134 New York. The Museum of Modern Art. *Yves Tanguy.* Exhibition. Catalogue by James Thrall Soby. New York, 1955; reprint, New York, Arno Press, 1972

135 Yves Tanguy. *Un recueil des ses oeuvres. A Summary of His Work,* by Kay Sage-Tanguy et al., New York, Pierre Matisse, distributed by Wittenborn, 1963

TANNING

136 Alain Bosquet. *La peinture de Dorothea Tanning.* Paris, J. J. Pauvert, 1966

INDEX